TEACHING THE FAITH

TEACHING THE FAITH

A guide to the modern presentation of traditional
catholic belief

LEONARD JOHNSTON

Sheed and Ward · London

First published 1973
This edition 1974
Sheed and Ward Ltd, 6 Blenheim St
London W1Y 0SA
© Leonard Johnston 1973
Nihil obstat: John M. T. Barton STD LSS *Censor*
Imprimatur: David Norris *Vicar General*
Westminster, 22 June 1973
Printed and bound in Great Britain by
REDWOOD BURN LIMITED
Trowbridge and Esher

Contents

Foreword for teachers

The ferment of thought on religious questions which has swept over the christian world in the last twenty years is exhilarating and exciting; but it has also left people anxious and uncertain. This uncertainty is particularly painful when it comes to education. Parents and teachers think with envy of their parents and teachers, who were able to give firm, clear answers to the serious questions on which the young quite rightly look to us for guidance. Now we sometimes wonder if there is anything certain we dare say.

But before pursuing this further, it may be useful to think again about our whole task, and what we are trying to do in religious education.

What are we trying to do?

The work of religious education can be described in many ways; but the one I would like to propose here is this – we are trying to help young christians to become mature persons.

First of all, we are 'helping': we are not engaged single-handed in a work in which our efforts alone will guarantee success or failure. It is in the first place God's work: 'Paul may sow, Apollo may water, but God makes it grow' (1 Cor 3:6). This does not relieve us, the educators, of all responsibility: but it does put our work into a certain context; it is a work of cooperation. Our part in this cooperation has many aspects: prompting, encouraging, guiding, inspiring. It also includes informing, giving information. This aspect of our work is not unimportant; indeed it may occupy the greater part of our time; but it is not an end in itself, only a means to an end.

This is further clarified by reflection on the persons we are dealing with – and especially by the realisation that they *are* persons. We are not dealing with inanimate material which we can mould to our will, we are not programming a computer. We are dealing with a person, a free being, capable of reason and responsibility. We can stimulate and guide a free being; we can even help him to see what his freedom is; we can help him to make a free choice; but we cannot impose a choice – ultimately, the choice is his.

It is presumed here that the persons we are dealing with are young christians; that is to say, not only free persons, but sons of God, already living with the life of Christ, with the light of the Holy Spirit already in them.

Some teachers may say that this is a very rash presumption; that many of the children we are dealing with, even in what is theoretically a christian school, come from the sort of background and environment which completely cuts them off from the remotest hint of christian influence. This is very often true. And yet, teachers know that this is much less true in young children. An anti-religious attitude is not natural to them; it is something they have to learn – something they *do* learn – from their environment, from society. But it is precisely the role of education to help to change society, to help the individual to master his environment. Moreover, the change we want to bring about is not something which is at odds with genuine humanity. Christianity is for all men: the whole point of the incarnation is that Christ has shown the way for all men to live. What we have to give is not something inhuman or anti-human, not something completely alien which we are forcing them to accept against all their instincts. We are trying to foster something which is already there, even though it may be in conflict with other elements in them and obstructed by other factors.

And we too, the teachers, are christians. As christians we have the common christian duty of sharing and caring for all men. This is the role of all christians, which each performs in whatever way he or she is called to. We are called to do it as members of the teaching profession, and our teaching of religion is simply the way in which we, as teachers, carry out our christian role of caring. If we were doctors, we would do it by our care for the sick; if we were bishops, we would do it by being bishops; since we are teachers, our teaching is our role in the body of Christ. And it is a recognised role: 'he has appointed in the church first apostles, second prophets, third teachers . . .' (1 Cor 12:28). We speak with the authority and the power of Christ behind us.

But these are young christians: and our task is to help them in their development. And once again, it is development, not mass-production of a finished article. There is a proper stage of development for the children here as there is in other branches of their education. A six-year old christian is different from an eleven-year old, and an eleven-year old from a sixteen-year old; and what is adequate at one stage of development may not be at another. It is wrong to cram young heads full of memorised facts, but it is equally wrong to leave an older child with an attitude to religion which would be dismissed as childish in other subjects.

The term of the development is described as 'mature persons'. This is of course partly to avoid a very complicated subject – there are dozens of ways of describing what we are aiming at; one could for example say that strictly speaking we want to produce saints – this is the only really successful result of religious training; or, as St Paul puts it, that we should become completely Christ-like, 'until we become the perfect man, fully mature with the fullness of Christ himself' (Eph 4:13). But to put it this way might seem rather ambitious for our prosaic efforts. Moreover, the phrase 'mature persons' is one way of drawing attention to the fact that the christian life covers the whole of life and involves every aspect of our being. Religious education is not a matter of developing one aspect of the person (called 'the soul' perhaps) while ignoring all others. It is part of the total education of the whole person. True, religious education will have its own specific contribution, its own insights into what is man's real character and destiny; but it is not in conflict with or isolated from other aspects of education. Our aim is to produce a mature person – one with a certain knowledge of himself and an integrated attitude to life, the world and society.

Many teachers find this a difficult and frightening task. It *is* difficult; all real teaching is arduous and demanding; so is any job which involves dealing with people, because people are not inanimate objects which stay put while we mould them as we want. It demands courage and perseverance and patience; it makes demands on our nervous energy which not all are willing to face. Some opt out of the profession; many more opt for a minimum of technical efficiency – they become instructors instead of teachers.

This is true of all teaching; but it is not more true of religious education than of other forms of teaching. The same techniques and skills apply here – the same methods of engaging the pupils' interest, stimulating, communicating and so on. Yet it does remain true that many teachers find this subject more frightening than any other.

There are various reasons one might suggest for this. One is that it certainly does bring out the quality in a teacher; the teacher who has settled for painless conveying of information will not really be a very good teacher anyway, but will find it virtually impossible in this subject which of its nature is concerned with personal formation. This is the ideal for all education; here, it is the whole point. On the other hand, some otherwise good teachers suffer from an exaggerated sense of responsibility on this point. 'Who could be qualified for this work?' they might be glad to hear St Paul saying; but Paul's own answer was that God simply wants us to do our best and he will look after the results. But in addition to this, there is here a misunderstanding of what religion is; and this we shall try to cope with in the next chapter.

But a much more common difficulty is the teacher's own uncertainty about what should be taught. This is especially true today when the comfortable certainties of the catechism seem to have been swept away, leaving the teacher not quite sure from day to day what is coming next, what is 'on' and what is 'off' and above all why it is so suddenly being changed. Teaching is a demanding enough task at the best of times, but it is a difficulty which any real teacher accepts gladly as a challenge to his skill and inspiration and sympathy. But it is an unfair burden to be asked to do it in an atmosphere of uncertainty about what should be done.

And that is what this book is about. It is not a book about reaching methods or hints on preparing classes. Good books do already exist which give help and suggestions specifically on teaching methods; and in any case most teachers of any professional competence would agree that they can work out their own methods if only they were clear on what to teach.

This book is an attempt to express the christian faith. The complaint about apparent changes in doctrine is a justified one. A church which claims to be teaching truth cannot swing round like a weathercock. But I hope to show that we are not in fact swinging round. But it is true that much of what has often been taught with cheerful assurance was not really an essential part of doctrine at all. One of the most disheartening phrases a theologian has to hear is, 'But I always thought . . . I was always taught that . . .' What follows may be any item from a sort of package deal which included pious custom, fanciful speculation, traditional opinion, a way of putting things which dates from long vanished thought-patterns – or a genuine expression of truth. Truth may not change; but our appreciation of it certainly does. Certainly we should not adopt change for the sake of change, merely following a fashion. But equally certainly no christian who believes in a living God, a God who is really with us now in our lives today would ever think that the fact that 'he always thought it' was proof against ever having to think again. This little book is an attempt to show the real meaning of what we really hold and why perhaps it may be better to put it this way today.

It really is a *little* book – a 'little faith' – (Mt 25:21). It must be. God wants all men to know him, to come to him – not only clever people with plenty of time to think things out. He can't possibly have made it so difficult that you need to be learned to see it. If it is difficult and complicated, it can't be essential. It is true that sometimes it takes time for us to get it clear – this may be true in the pages which follow – but at the end, it must be simple.

1

Religion and revelation

Much of the confusion, difficulty and misunderstanding about religion springs not so much from difficulties about individual doctrines as from a misunderstanding of the whole subject. Religion is a personal relationship to a personal God.

God is a person. When we describe God as first uncaused cause, or the supreme being who alone exists of himself, or any of the other familiar definitions of God, we are saying something certainly; but we are passing over the most important point – that God is not a powerful machine or a super-computer, not an object, not a thing, but a person.

The idea of 'personality' is rich in meaning, and we shall be saying more about it in the next chapter; but here we are concentrating on one aspect; a person is one who communicates.

God communicates

If you are in a room by yourself, and you suddenly hear the word 'hullo', you don't say, 'what's that?'; you say 'Who's there?', because you know that it is only a person who can speak; you know it is not the noise of the rain on the window or the creaking of the furniture; it is not something, it is someone. Moreover, you would say 'Who's there', or something like that: you wouldn't go on eating your supper or reading the

1

paper, merely registering the fact that someone spoke. When someone speaks it is natural to reply. Because just as it is a person who communicates, so the one with whom he communicates is a person. You sometimes hear the exasperated remark, when there is no reply, 'I may as well be talking to the wall'. The point is that you would not normally talk to a wall; you would not expect any reply from it; but you do expect a response from a person.

In the act of communication two persons make contact. To communicate is to express oneself; to speak is literally to give oneself away, to open up to someone. What is really being communicated is one's self. It is not primarily a matter of conveying information; it is a very dull and 'uncommunicative' person who speaks only when he has some message to give. Most of our conversation consists of quite trivial and casual remarks (things like, 'How are you', to which we do not really expect a factual answer); they are really just signals and counters expressing our willingness to make contact. In fact much of our communication takes place without words – a smile, a frown, a handshake; these are ways in which we communicate. Communication means just what it says: a communion of persons.

And when we say that God is a person, this is what we mean; we mean that he expresses himself, he enters into communication with us, he invites us to share his personality. His communication is his self-expression – he communicates with us in all the ways in which he expresses himself; in creation, in the whole world around us, in human life, in history; and most completely and perfectly, in Christ.

We call this 'revelation'. This word is often used as if it referred to items of information that God conveys to us – the Trinity is a 'revelation', the real presence is a 'revelation' and so on. But revelation means first of all

God's revelation of himself: 'God revealed himself and divine truths . . .', as Vatican II puts it. He reveals himself first; that is the point. What lies at the heart of revelation and religion is not an information system, but a person who enters into communication with us.

Faith: *response to God's communication*

Our response to God revealing is called 'faith'. There is probably no religious concept so riddled with confusion as this. This is partly due to the fact that the word is used in a variety of ways referring to different attitudes; but it is mainly due to the initial misunderstanding of revelation. 'Revelation' and 'faith' are correlative terms. So if you take 'revelation' to mean conveying information, then naturally 'faith' is taken to mean accepting that information. Then if 'faith' means knowing some information the question arises, 'How do you know it?'. Do you prove it (in the same way as you prove that an equilateral triangle has equal angles), or do you just take it 'on faith'? And if it is the former, how is it faith, how does it differ from knowledge? And if it is the latter, is it not an irrational act? A good many people almost unconsciously accept an illogical compromise; you try to prove as much as you can – and when reason fails you call it a 'mystery' and take it on faith.

Then again, if 'faith' means knowing things, it tends to make religion into a science consisting of a list of data – if you know these facts you 'have the faith'; if you get one wrong, you are a heretic. And then again, the list itself becomes in a way more important than the meaning. We say: 'Is it on the list? is it an article of faith? is it a dogma? If so, then of course I will believe it, even if I do not understand it'. There must be many good christians who recite the creed in all sincerity, and who firmly profess their faith that God is one and

3

God is three, but who have never asked themselves what this is about, what is the point of it, what meaning it has in our lives.

These are just some of the difficulties which arise when 'revelation' is taken to mean giving information and 'faith' as knowing this information. These difficulties are not insoluble. Take, for example, that difficulty about 'believing or proving': one would naturally point out that there are many things in life which have to be taken on faith, and this is not unreasonable provided that you can trust the person whose authority you are accepting. I am not denying the role of reason in religion; on the contrary, it is very important that we should be able to see the coherence between our religious attitudes and our normal ways of thinking. Nor am I suggesting that faith is not concerned with facts at all. God does reveal 'himself *and* divine truths', just as when you know a friend, you not only know him, but you also know all sorts of things about him – you have greater insight into his character, his motives, his reactions and so on. But I am saying that to treat religion as if it were primarily a matter of knowing and proving is to approach the subject in a wrong way. It is to use the wrong tool for the job. We use different tools for different jobs; we approach different subjects in different ways. Just as you could not use a knife for knitting, so you would not apply mathematics to a work of literature; you would not consider it a fair test of a book to say how big it is. Nor would you use chemical analysis as a test of a painting, judging it by measuring the various pigments used. And in the same way, you do not judge a person as if he were a thing; you do not approach it as if it were a mathematical problem. A person is not something you prove. A person is someone you either know or do not know, someone you have met or have not met, someone with whom you communicate. And revelation is communication with the person who is God. To ask then whether faith is something you can prove or something you have to take on trust is a false question. It is like asking whether you can really prove that a Beethoven symphony is a great work of art. You either appreciate it or not; it appeals to you or it does not; it speaks to you or it does not (not perhaps all at once, but gradually). Faith is insight, faith is the ability to hear (an ability which goes far beyond the physical gift of hearing); faith is sympathy; faith is appreciation; faith is the response to God who speaks to us not in words but in the world, in our lives, in people, in Christ.

Religion: communication and response

The whole idea – and the whole of religion – is summed up succinctly and strongly in those words of St John: 'God so loved the world that he gave his Son so that we might live.' Those dozen words contain all that is essential. It tells us what we mean by God; that he is a person. It tells us what sort of a person he is, that he 'loves'; that the mark of his love is seen in his giving; when he created the world, he was giving – giving it a share in his own existence; when he made man in his own image and likeness, he was giving himself, and the climax of his giving was Christ. In Jesus, God gave himself to us totally and unreservedly; and the purpose of this is our good, our life, ultimately a share in his own life.

Perhaps those who find much in the modern approach to the teaching of religion which is disturbing would find even in this simple point some illumination. Does it not explain, for example, why there appears to be a lack of concern with doctrinal formulations, less insistence on the children learning off set answers? It is because it is felt that our concern should be with 'introducing' the children to our Lord;

5

to fostering that personal relationship with God which was implanted in them by baptism, and giving scope for the working of the Holy Spirit who is undoubtedly present in us. Not that doctrinal formulation and catechism answers are irrelevant. This is really a matter for the teacher to decide by personal experience. But whatever the teacher decides, it should be recognised that the formulae are not an end in themselves, though they may be the means by which the personal relationship is formed, made explicit and developed. It is not some sort of spiritual examination that we are preparing the children for, but for growth as sons of God.

Religion and education

But if we think of revelation like this – as God reaching out to us, offering himself to us, entering into communication with us, then there is an even more far-reaching consequence, one which affects our whole attitude to religion and the teaching of it. It means that the term 'religion' is not a universal term, with one clearly defined meaning. It is a term which has a whole range of meanings. Or to put it another way, it is a reality which is expressed at different levels of completeness.

To explain this more fully, let us go back to our basic idea; that God enters into communication with men; he communicates himself to us in the world around us, he communicates himself in the very being of man made in his image, he communicates himself to us in history, he communicates himself in Christ.

But if this is what God is doing, then what is needed on our part if we are to receive his communication is an attitude of openness, of receptivity, of awareness. But this is what all educators (teachers and parents) are trying to foster. When a mother encourages and guides the baby's uncertain gropings, when the growing child explores the world in which we live (under the guise of history, geography, science and so on), when a young person falls in love even; all of these are manifestations of that attitude of openness and awareness which is a rudimentary form of the religious attitude. This attitude of openness and reaching out is directed to various objects – to joy, to knowledge, to beauty, to truth, to love, to persons; and God is in them all. If – and when – this attitude reaches a recognition that these values are embodied in a personal power outside oneself, this is another stage of religion. And it is yet another stage when we recognise this personal power, whom we may now call 'God', as one who reaches out to us; as one who has entered into communication with us in history (the God of the bible); and most of all in Jesus of Nazareth. And yet another stage is reached when we recognise Jesus of Nazareth not merely as a great figure in history, but as the one in whom the destiny of mankind reaches its fulfilment, one whom we can therefore call 'messiah' (see pp 28f) and one who lives now and personally influences our present existence – this is christianity. We may then ponder the implications of this phrase, 'influencing our existence'; realise that he is the starting point and source of a new sort of existence, a new community, something which we can call a church; realise that what we call religion is a life lived out in that association. And we may also come to recognise that Christ and the life he has made available to us is the complete expression of all our ideals, of all our existence; that our whole being should be more and more permeated by his Spirit, until we can say that we live now, not ourselves, but Christ lives in us.

What we call 'religion', then, spans the whole range of human attitudes from the first struggles to be really human to the total dedication to the work of the Spirit in us which results in our transformation into a divine being. All these are valid meanings of the term 'religion.' It means that no one who is trying to be human at all is completely without religion; and it means that none of us is sufficiently religious till the day we die.

And from the point of view of religious education, it means that the work of religious education is really the task of education itself. If we care about people at all, if we care about children, if we are interested in helping them to be truly human, then we are teaching religion in some sense. It is a truism that every teacher is a teacher of English; it is even more true that every teacher is a teacher of religion. The difference between religious education and other branches of education lies not so much in the subject taught as in the insight of the person teaching it. If God has offered himself to us in history, in our environment, in human experience, then it is dealing with these that we find God revealing himself to us. To say anything else is to make God just one subject amongst others, along with geography, history, biology and the rest.

At a slightly more technical level, it means that the proper way to teach religion is in an integrated curriculum. Educationalists may argue about the advantages and disadvantages of 'the integrated day' but for religion this is not merely an academic debate, but the method appropriate to the subject.

But it should be noted: (a) that this is proposed as a matter of principle, not as a rule of practice; it is the attitude that the teacher should have. How it should be expressed in practice – whether special religious lessons should be abolished, or how the syllabus should be integrated – are obviously not subjects to be dealt with here. (b) We are talking about religious *education* in the sense discussed above; a much stronger case could be made for special lessons of religious instruction – information about religion. (c) The place of

Christ is central; when we say that the term 'religion' has several different levels of meaning, we do not imply that all these meanings are equal. In Christ the whole of religion is expressed perfectly; in him God communicates himself perfectly, and at the same time the human response to this communication is expressed in him most perfectly.

Finally, it also means this: that we can deal with any human being at the level at which we find them, and nourish that which they have – that we do not have to take any one level of religion and try to foist it on to everyone regardless of where they stand. It would be wrong to propose theological subtleties to adolescents still struggling to sort out their human values; and it would be equally wrong to deprive a christian child in a christian environment of some glimpse of the glory that is open to us. There is no one standard that is equally valid for everyone always. But what is true for everyone, always, is that the teaching of religion is an invitation, a challenge, a summons, an appeal – to seek, to grow, to be, to go onwards, to be continually leaving behind, to find ourselves, to make ourselves, to strive towards the infinite ocean of life and love that is God.

2

God

The first difficulty about this subject is just that: that we are tempted to deal with it as if it were an academic subject, as if it were a slightly complicated bit of mathematics. We talk about proving the existence of God in much the same way that a scientist was prepared to prove the existence of the meson particle. And books on christian doctrine go on to deduce the qualities and characteristics of this being – that he is omnipotent, that he is everywhere, and so on (all of them, incidentally, instead of making him more real, making it more and more difficult to visualise him or to think of him as a real person).

All of this affects very much our attitude to the doctrine of the Trinity. 'Person' and 'nature' become counters to be manipulated, and once you have them right – three of one to one of the other – you have all you need on the subject.

But God is a person. Actually, I would prefer to say that God is a personal being, simply in order to avoid giving the impression that he is a person in exactly the same way as we are (so that the Trinity, for example, is thought of as 'three people'). He is at any rate not a thing, not an impersonal power. He is a personal being; he is in fact the first person, the source of personality, who calls us to be persons in relationship to him.

10

By 'person' we mean a being endowed with freedom and intelligence. But there is another aspect of personality which has been stressed more in recent years, and that is its social connotation.

Personality is only really expressed in relationship with another. Sometimes the word 'personal' is used to stress that which belongs to somebody exclusively, that which marks him off from others: 'This is my personal property', we say, meaning that it belongs to me and to no one else; or, 'He has a very personal point of view', meaning that his point of view is different from anyone else's. But it might be better to use the word 'individual' in such statements. 'Individual' and 'person' are often used as if they were synonymous, but more properly 'individual' denotes that which marks someone off from others, whereas 'personality' is the quality by which we are related to others. You can use the word 'individual' of any separate member of any group – an individual cow in a herd, for example, or an individual blade of grass. But you can only use the word 'person' of individuals who can communicate with each other. Of course there must be something there to communicate; but it is in the act of communicating that this something becomes aware of itself. It's rather like one's awareness of one's own body. If you close your eyes and put one hand behind your back, you can't really be sure that you can feel the other hand. You can feel the air on your skin and the blood in your veins; but it's a very different feeling from when you slap your hand on the table. Then you really feel not only the table but your hand. So it is in the act of communicating with another person that we become aware of our own personality, that we assert it and develop it.

And men are persons in relationship to God. Man is

11

'responsible' – that is to say, he can respond. God's communication and man's response are expressed in the world in which we live. The bible describes creation in terms of 'speaking': 'God said, Let there be light'. This is a way of expressing the idea that the universe is not the product of blind chance but bears the impress of an intelligible will. And man too, made in God's image and likeness, can make the world into an intelligible situation.

Man is responsible; he is free. He is not a programmed computer who can only parrot mindlessly what he is told to say. The relationship between God and man is a real dialogue, a real exchange of free beings. 'The will of God' – the expression and the idea – is often used as if God had each man's life mapped out for him. But surely this cannot be so. God waits on man; that is to say, he speaks and then waits for man's free response, and the resulting dialogue is what makes a man a person in relationship to God.

This does not deny or infringe God's supremacy. Take the example of two men sitting down to play chess, one a grand master and the other a novice with only the simplest knowledge of the elementary rules of the game. There is no doubt at all who is going to win the game; but the master can't do anything until the novice has made his move.

Mystery

This analogy has its weakness; any analogy has. We are after all dealing with a mystery here. But let us be careful too about this word 'mystery'. We sometimes use it as an excuse for the failure of reason; in trying to grasp the idea of the Trinity, for example, we do our best, but when we reach the limits of understanding without having made very much progress we say, with combined exasperation and relief, 'Well after all, it is a mystery'. But this is not what the word 'mystery' means. The word is used in a variety of ways but the idea of mysteriousness or unknowability is the least important of them. In the bible it is used simply to describe God's plan for the world, a plan which is unrolled step by step throughout successive ages: 'He has let us know the mystery of his purpose, the hidden plan he made in Christ from the beginning to act when the times had run their course' (Eph 1:9). This of course means that until God has shown his hand, it is going to be hidden, secret, 'mysterious'; and Paul's claim is that in Christ the essence of God's plan has been made plain: 'The knowledge of the mystery has been revealed to me – it was unknown to men of previous generations – that pagans now share our promises through Christ' (Eph 3:4-6). But he also recognises that there is still much more to be worked out in God's good time – why, for example, there is still evil in the world even though Christ has conquered (2 Thes 2:7) is part of God's unfolding plan, part of 'the mystery'.

But this plan is worked out in human life, and the word 'mystery' is also then used to describe this association between the divine and the human. Paul uses it in this way when he describes marriage as 'a mystery' – because in the association between man and woman God's association with the human race is represented. We use it in this sense too when we speak of 'the mysteries of the rosary'; there is nothing particularly baffling about, for example, Mary's visit to her cousin Elizabeth; but when we say it is 'a mystery' we mean that there is more in it than meets the eye, we mean that it is an incident in which God's dealings with men are represented.

But this last links with another way in which the word 'mystery' can be used. There are two things which it is hard to see. One is an object which is far away – like an airplane high in the sky, or a single tree on a distant mountain. But it is equally difficult to see something which is too close to us; if you hold your hand up in front of your eyes and gradually move it closer, it eventually becomes just a blur. And similarly it is not only the things that are above us which are mysterious, but even more those which are too close to us. This is true of all the really important elements in our human situation – life, love, death, and so on; we cannot fully grasp them or explain them, not because they are remote from us but on the contrary because they are too close to us. We are involved in them, so that trying to understand them is like trying to use a pair of scissors to cut the scissors with. And the same is true of our relationship with God. It is not merely because he is so far above the scope of our minds that we find him impossible to grasp fully, but also because he is too close to us, part of our very being.

But then perhaps a lot of our theology fails by attempting to deal with God as if one could relate to him in an objective, impersonal way; and then of course we do have to fall back on the word 'mystery' as an excuse for the fact that this doesn't take us very far. But it doesn't take us very far not because it is mysterious but because we are tackling it in the wrong way. Let me try a little parable. There was once a goldfish which happily spent its days swimming round and round its bowl. Then one day it occurred to the little goldfish that it didn't really know very much about its situation or what it was doing or where it was going: 'For all I know', said the little goldfish, 'I might just be swimming round in circles'. So it decided that the thing to do was to take a good look at the situation, to be completely objective about it, to look at itself from the outside. So it flipped outside the bowl; and what was left was one empty bowl and one dead goldfish. If we are dealing with something in which we ourselves are involved, we are doomed to failure if we try to deal with it by removing ourselves from it, if we try to deal with it in an objective or impersonal way. God is a person with whom we are in personal relationship; we can only approach him through this personal relationship.

Personal relationship

This may cast light on (and be illuminated by) a difficulty which teachers often meet from children, and feel slightly frustrated when they can't answer simply. We tell the children that God is everywhere; and then the children ask: 'Is he sitting on my chair? Do I stand on him when I walk?' and so on. But God is not the sort of being who can be 'in a place' any more than when you say 'I have an idea in my head' it can actually be discovered by a craniotomy. A personal relationship is not the same as a relationship of place. If I am sitting in a railway compartment with another person, each of us immersed in our own thoughts, both deep in our newspapers, never speaking to each other or even looking at each other; are we really in personal contact? It might just as well be a sack of potatoes in the other corner for all the difference it makes. We are close to each other physically, 'near' each other in place; but we are not at all near to each other as persons. Whereas if I have a friend in New York and telephone him, we are three thousand miles apart physically, but we are in very close personal contact. But God is not only a person – he is nothing else but personality, he is pure personality; and he can be in very close personal relationship with us without being bound to physical closeness. He made us; he upholds us in being; he calls us to be like him; he can even use physical means to make contact with us (like the telephone in the example above); but to say that he is in this or that place is not so much false as the wrong sort of language[1].

15

God is a person, with whom we are in a personal relationship. When we are trying to think about God, it is in terms of personal relationships that we should be thinking about him. Theology is not like mathematics. A better analogy for theology, and for the teaching of religion, would be art. You do not discuss a painting in terms of quantity, as if you could judge its quality by its size. In any form of art, it is a question of appreciation, of trying to relate to the artist's vision expressed through his particular medium. But even more, theology should be treated like a personal relationship, a willing compenetration of another person communicating with us.

This, finally, gives us also a way of approach to the very heart of the divine mystery, the Trinity. God is a person; or rather he is a personal being; but now through Christ we know that he is a three-personal being. We have already noted how this is sometimes treated as if it were simply a non-rational piece of information. But if we approach the mystery from the point of view of personality and in particular from the point of view of personal relationship with us, then it seems to be more meaningful.

We begin simply with God – this personal power beyond ourselves. But though he is beyond us in some sense, he is also the very ground of our being, and of all being. He is not a static force; he is living, alive, acting, outgoing, outpouring; he is what lies at the source and goal of our own urgent, creative life. This aspect of God can be, has been, described in various ways – all simply attempts to express something of the vital and dynamic reality. We say that he is creator; we say that he is a communicator, that he speaks; that he is a giver, one who sends, a lover. No matter how described, this activity of God sets up a relationship with us; and this relationship too can be described in various ways, but the way we have been taught to use by preference is the relationship between father and son. In this relationship with God, then, as loving source of our being, we speak of him as Father.

But God's action is not just from outside; he is not a person who stands above us, thundering down commands from the height of his heaven, dabbling with the human situation while himself keeping his distance. When he communicates, he communicates himself; when he gives, he gives himself. And Christ is the one in whom God has communicated himself totally. God is a giver; Christ is the gift. God is a sender; Christ is the one who is sent. God is a speaker; Christ is the word. God is a Father; Christ is the Son. But because God gives himself to us totally in Jesus, and because Jesus shares our being, we are now related to the one God in a new way; and in this relationship we know him as our brother, God the Son.

But even this is not enough. He does not stand above us and outside us, but comes and shares our being. Now in addition, he – this same, only, God – then makes it possible for us to share his being. He is not only by our side, he is within us. The result of God's self-communication, the result of his sharing of our life, is the transformation of our life, and the setting up of yet another relationship; and in this relationship to God who is our life we speak of him as God the Spirit[2].

God is not a doctrine, but a person; and a person who can be spoken of only as a relationship which is lived; but finally, it is a three-fold relationship which we live; from him, through him and in him.

Notes
1 May I repeat that this is an attempt to explain the theology; it is not an attempt to change accepted habits of speech. So it is quite normal in christian tradition to say that God is 'in heaven' or that he is 'in our souls'; and it would be impossible to speak at all without using such language. But it might help us if we were more clearly aware of the real meaning and the limitations of this

metaphorical language.

2 For those who are interested in the niceties of theological discourse, I hasten to add that this account is lacking in one respect at least. It deals with the relationships only from our point of view, whereas of course God is expressed in three persons even apart from us, before man and time began.

But in the first place, it has already been explained that this is an attempt to make doctrine meaningful, to put it in a way which a teacher would have a good chance of adapting to the understanding of children; and this seems to be worth doing even at the expense of some risk, rather than leaving a completely impenetrable block of doctrine, a dark 'mystery'.

In the second place, is this way of putting it really as inaccurate as it might appear? It is good thomistic teaching that the personality of the three divine persons consists in a relationship (cf *Summa Theologiae* 1. 28, especially art 2); and it is easy to see how the relationships described above can be traced back to the nature of God himself. Karl Rahner (*The Trinity*, New York 1970) would go even further; cf for example, p 21: 'There *must* be a connexion between Trinity and man. The Trinity is a mystery of *salvation*. . . . The "economic" Trinity (the Trinity in relationship to man) *is* the "immanent" Trinity (the Trinity in God himself)'.

What think you of Christ ?

This is literally the crucial question, for all christians as well as for the teacher of religion. This is not just a dogma amongst others; this is the centre of our christian life, and ultimately, we may come to see, of our human life, of our life as persons. This is the criterion of success or failure. If we are to judge our lives successful, this is what success is, 'to know the one true God and the Son he has sent' (Jn 17:3) If we fail, it is 'because we have not believed in the only-begotten Son' (Jn 3:18). We have already spoken about God, the person who calls us to be persons; but it is only because of *this* person, Jesus, that we are able to speak of God: 'No one has ever seen God; the only-begotten Son has revealed him' (Jn 1:18); there is no other way to the Father except through him (Jn 14:6).

This has always been recognised by christians; and it is as true now as ever it was. But it is not something we simply accept unthinkingly. A christian strives unceasingly to understand our Lord better, to penetrate more deeply into the mystery of Jesus.

Our efforts at penetration must begin with the humanity of our Lord. When he says, 'There is no other way to the Father except by me', it is of the visible, physical reality standing in front of his hearers that he is speaking. 'The Word has become flesh'; not appeared as flesh, or pretended to be flesh; but the Word, God's self-revelation, was totally conveyed to us in the physical reality of Jesus. 'The fullness of divinity dwells in him in bodily form' (Col 2:9).

This is the divinely authorised method of procedure, to begin with our Lord known to us as a man; but it is also our human way. The process of understanding takes place by identification and assimilation; by identifying ourselves with the subject, by trying to find something in it with which we can identify, and working from that similarity. In any subject, not just this one, we can only understand when there is something in common between us and the subject we are dealing with, something to grasp hold of, something to make contact with. Of course as the process goes on it should make a difference to the subject knowing as well; but it begins with something we have in common with the object known. For example, if I happen to be an Englishman of a certain age and a certain background, I am in a good position to understand other middle-aged, middle-class Englishmen. If it is an English woman, I am going to find it slightly more difficult and we can make contact only through what we do have in common, not through the difference of sex which divides us; in fact, the only chance I have of understanding her as a woman is by starting with the factors we have in common. If I happen to be talking to a Frenchman, it is going to be rather more difficult, but at least we have a certain amount of experience in common, we both have a European background. If it is a Chinese teenager I am dealing with, this is obviously going to be much more difficult; it's not only the relatively simple difficulty of language, but even supposing one of us knew the other's language very well, there is still the question of mental background, the undertones to the words we use, the presuppositions. But at least we are both men; we do not belong to different planets or different species; and at least as fellow members of the human race we can make contact.

In trying to understand our Lord, then, it is here that we must begin, with what we have in common, with our common experience of humanity.

And our Lord is a human being, a historical figure; one who was accessible to his contemporaries at the human level, and to us through their testimony. He came from an ordinary working-class family but became something of a public figure as a speaker, a teacher, with all the talents of a teacher and public speaker richly at his command. He coined epigrams; he told stories that held his audience and also had as a sort of after-taste a pungent little point; coined *bon mots* – 'wolves in sheep's clothing'; 'let the dead bury their dead'; 'whited sepulchres'; 'it's not what goes into a man that defiles, but what comes out of him'; 'faith can move mountains' – so copiously that he is more quoted than anyone but Shakespeare. He could burst out into passages of impassioned rhetoric especially in denunciation of hypocrisy (think of that glorious passage with its repeated 'Woe to you, scribes and pharisees, hypocrites . . . you who strain at a fly and swallow a camel . . . you who won't go through the door and won't let anyone else go through . . .'). This too is striking – how unabashed he is by authority; anyone else in his position, with no formal education and no official position, might well have felt a little ill-at-ease faced with men of recognised scholarship and training, and might have been excused or even commended for deferring to them, or else he might have over-reacted with a touch of bravado or aggressiveness. But this man was the same with rich and poor, with learned men and the unlettered crowds. He could disarm his critics, he could literally reduce them to silence. He was indeed gentle and considerate, but he was also strong and fearless. Many of his ideas were revolutionary, some of them politically, others so extraordinary that they could only be expressed as paradox ('count yourself lucky when people are against you'); yet he never presented the conventional picture of a revolutionary. He was unconventional, but not eccentric; he was completely self-possessed, but not self-contained or introvert. You might sum it up by saying that he was free: free from convention, free from authority, free from fear, free from pettiness, free from idiosyncracy, free from self-seeking, free from boasting, free from compromise. He was completely his own man; and yet a man for all men, a man for all seasons.

And all of this is not even to mention the strange powers and miraculous deeds attributed to him. The impression we get, reading the account left to us by his contemporaries, is that these were almost incidental, almost taken for granted given the kind of man he was. It was this, his personality, which struck people – the magnetism which could make him be taken seriously when he said, this Galilean workman: 'Follow me . . . Take up your cross and follow me'.

A strange, compelling figure; yet real – there was no doubt about that. His friends walked with him, talked with him, had meals with him, knew something of his family, knew him in joy and sorrow, in triumph and doubt and fear. They really knew him; and yet always they felt that there was something about him which went beyond what they saw.

And in their attempt to grasp it, the process of understanding described above is at work. They try to fit him into some context or category with which they are already familiar. They stand before Jesus and say, 'What is he like? Like what sort of person we already know?' In doing this, in trying to find some common ground or basis of comparison, naturally they look first of all to their own religious tradition, to the old testament. Naturally, and rightly; Jesus himself belonged to the same tradition and the way he thought about himself and presented himself followed the same lines.

From the old testament they draw on many different ideas which help them to 'situate' Jesus, which make it possible for them to think about him intelligibly; and these images they present to us, as suitable ways in which we too may think about Jesus[1].

All of these different images have some contribution to make to our understanding of Jesus; out of them all we will merely select two for fuller consideration. But before doing so, we shall try to see the starting point of their thinking

The starting point

Our Lord's death was a traumatic experience for those friends of his who had followed him, learned to know him, admire him, love him; for whom he had become the centre of existence. We can feel something of this in the words of two of them talking to the mysterious stranger who asked them, the day after it happened, why they were looking so sad: 'Because of Jesus of Nazareth', they said, 'A prophet mighty in word and deed before God and all the people. The authorities condemned him to death and had him crucified. We thought he was the one who was going to redeem Israel . . .' (Lk 24:19-21). This was the tragic end to all their hopes − until they realised that he had risen from the dead. This was not just the miracle of coming back from the dead. For them, for all the Jews, life was not just a biological phenomenon, the state of not being dead; it was a gift from God, a share in the life of God himself. They described this life metaphorically as 'the breath of God' or 'the spirit of God'. One of the earliest descriptions of the creation of man gives us the idea: 'God breathed into man's nostrils the breath of life, and he became a living being'.

If then Jesus came back to life after dying, then

surely he must have life, the spirit of God, to an extra-ordinary degree, to be able to conquer death itself. This is what Peter proclaimed on the first feast of Pentecost: 'Jesus has been raised, and has received the promised Spirit' (Ac 2:33). Moreover, the apostles found in this an explanation of their own strange experience that same day: 'He has received the promised Spirit and has poured it out, as you see and hear' (Ac 2:33). And then – their minds go back to the life of Jesus before he died – does this not explain so much about him which had puzzled them then? It was by the power of the Spirit that he did the things he did and above all spoke as he did, with authority. A man possessed by the Spirit of God – that's what Jesus was.

But here they are on familiar ground, here they have a context in which they can think Jesus. Because they are acquainted with the idea of men who were filled with the Spirit of God to do great things and to speak God's word. They called them prophets.

Prophet

The idea of the word of God, of God communicating with them, was familiar to the Israelites; not as an audible sound nor even simply as an idea addressed to their understanding; their idea of God's communication was something that God did, and they had experienced it in their history. It was a word which calls, as when Abraham was summoned to leave his father's house and his home-land; in the exodus they knew it as a word which saves, which creates, which gives new life; a word which in the law imperiously summoned men to live according to the life they had been called to. In all these different ways, God's word came to them. But when God spoke through the prophets, his word took the form of a human word. It came to men through human lips, formed and formulated in a

24

human mind and addressed to men in the normal forms of human speech. The prophets were not depersonalised by their prophetic role, not cast into a trance, deprived of sense and feeling. They spoke with free intelligence, and the influence of their particular environment and their individual personalities shows through their speeches. 'The word has become flesh' would be an intelligible statement to an Israelite. But this does not mean that the words of the prophets were simply their own words, expressing their own ideas and opinions. It was still God's word they uttered and it came from them with the same authority and effective power as it did when God communicated with men in thunder and earthquake: 'Is not my word a fire', says Jeremiah, 'a hammer that shatters the rocks' (Jer 23:29). God did not reduce the prophets to mindless automata, but he did enter into their very minds and hearts. They bear the word of God, they carry it. They not only speak the word that God commanded them to speak, but they experience it, they live it, they act it. We see this in a passage of one of the prophets (Is 8:18) where he says: 'I and the children God has given me are signs and portents to Israel'. His children were given curious-sounding names which were symbolic of the fate which was to come on Israel because of her sins: *Shear Jashub*, meaning 'a remnant will remain', and *Mahershalal-hash-baz*, meaning 'make haste to the spoil, speed to the prey'. These children play no further part in history; they don't say anything, they don't do anything, the prophet never refers to them directly; but the mere fact that they exist and that they are his sons makes them part of the prophet's message. And the same is true of the prophet himself; he not only acts as a prophet, so to speak – he *is* a prophet, and his whole existence is a message, a 'sign' to Israel. We see this again in two other incidents in two of the other prophets. To Jeremiah, God says: 'You must not

25

take a wife or have son or daughter' (Jer 16:1). Just that. The message is that the country is to be invaded and men will see their wives and children killed; but the significant point is that the prophet is not asked merely to say this – he is asked to experience it. The message is in his life, in his own experience of barrenness and childlessness. The same point emerges from another passage which is best read just as it stands: 'Son of man, I am about to deprive you suddenly of the light of your eyes. But you are not to lament nor weep nor go into mourning. I told this to the people in the morning; and my wife died in the evening' (Ez 24:15-18). Again, the prophet lives out his message that Israel, apple of God's eye, espoused by him in love, is to be taken into captivity, but since this is the punishment of her infidelity, it is not to be received with sympathy or grief.

What makes these examples particularly significant is the fact that they are prophecies of adversity. For the word of God very often is laden with doom. Not that God delights in catastrophe for its own sake or takes pleasure in spreading gloom. But men are called to a high ideal, and when they are not living up to this ideal what can the prophet do but urge on them the consequences of their actions; what would be the point of his offering false assurance, 'crying "peace" when there is no peace'? So the prophet's message is about disaster; and he lives it in his own life.

The climax of this is reached in the thought of one writer of the bible who speaks of a good servant of the Lord, endowed with the spirit of the Lord, who preaches with love and gentleness ('he does not crush the bruised reed nor quench the wavering flame', Is 42:1-4), but meets with scorn and opposition and is finally put to death. But his death is really living out the fate of the nation: 'A man of sorrows familiar with suffering; but ours were the sufferings he bore, ours the sorrows he carried. He was pierced for our faults and crushed for our sins'. But the inspiration of this prophet goes far beyond the realisation that sin is punished by suffering, and that the prophet may be asked to bear this message in his own life. He sees that suffering may also bring about atonement for sin, and that the prophet's suffering may have this value too. 'On him lies the punishment that brings us peace and through his wounds we are healed' (Is 53: 3-5).

All of this is what the old testament meant by 'a prophet'; so that when the new testament calls Jesus a prophet, this is not a mere title of respect or a reference to the fact that he was a great preacher. Still less, of course, is it a reference to the fact that he foretold the future; this is a very minor and incidental aspect of prophecy in the bible. It is a very meaningful title, and one which gives us real insight into the mystery of his being.

It means, at the simplest level, that we recognise him as the greatest of that line of spiritual geniuses who spoke in the power of the spirit. We recognise him as one who spoke with authority because he was sent by God. We recognise that the word of God came to men through him – that word of God which creates, calls, summons, saves; that word of God which offers men a share in God's own being which we call a covenant; it is in Jesus that this word comes to men.

But it means too that we realise that this word is embodied in him; that he not only speaks the word but lives it; this mighty word of God is seen not only in his words but in his deeds. We remember how the disciples on the road to Emmaus told the stranger who joined them about 'Jesus, a prophet mighty in word and in deed' (Lk 24:19); and we remember that it was not only after his speaking but after his great deeds like the raising of the widow's son that the crowds cry out, 'A great prophet has arisen among us' (Lk 7:16). The

27

word of God had shown itself in many different ways; but Jesus himself is the fullest expression and embodiment of it, 'the word made flesh'.

But this concept of prophet helps us, as it helped his first followers, to understand also what they found most bewildering – the tragedy of his death. Our reflection on the prophets brought home to us that 'the word of God is a two-edged sword' (Heb 4:12); it is a rebuke and a challenge to our lives. For that reason the prophets who bring the word of God must meet with opposition, resentment and even persecution ('which of the prophets did your fathers not persecute', Ac 7:52).This helps us to understand how Jesus too was 'a sign of contradiction' (Lk 2:34), and why he met with opposition and persecution. He was a prophet, and this was the fate that a prophet had to expect. But, finally, *this* prophet not only told men that sin leads to death; he also expressed it in deed, in his body: 'he bore our sufferings, he carried our sorrows; he was pierced for our sins, crushed for our faults' (Is 53: 4-5). And then he rose from the dead; and this too is a prophecy in action – his resurrection is a message of hope for us too: 'Through his wounds we are healed . . . By his sufferings my servant justifies many, taking their faults upon himself' (Is 53: 5,11)

Messiah

What do you think of Jesus? How are we to think of him? 'Thou art the Christ', said Peter (Mk 8:29); 'Jesus is the Christ', was Paul's first reaction to the revelation on the Damascus road (Ac 9:22); and Peter's first proclamation to the people at Pentecost was this, 'Let all the house of Israel know that God has made him Lord and Christ'. This has become so fundamental to our understanding of Jesus that it has become almost a proper name, 'Jesus Christ'; and his

28

followers call themselves by this name above all, 'christians'.

'Christ', of course, is simply the Greek translation of the Hebrew 'messiah', meaning 'the anointed one' – a title which goes back to David.

David was the first real king in Israel, and his reign marks a turning point in the history of the nation. Before him, Israel was an uncertain confederation of tribes struggling for existence – and struggling too, when David arrived, with no great prospect of success. David completely transformed this situation. He defeated their enemies and brought them freedom and victory, and in so doing knit them together into a single nation, a successful and flourishing kingdom.

This was certainly a wonderful achievement, and for this alone David would rightly hold a place of honour in the memories of his people. But there was still more to it than that. Israel was not simply a political creation; it was a nation whose principle of unity was its relationship with God – what we call the covenant. This meant that in addition to this political and military achievement, David also had to guide the nation through a crisis of identity; he had to bring about the necessary political and social development in such a way as to maintain continuity with the older and more fundamental principle of the covenant. Briefly, this was achieved by recognising the king as the embodiment and personification of the nation – and therefore of its covenant status. The covenant was not abandoned, its force as the binding link in the life of the community was not displaced by the monarchy; the covenant status of the nation as a whole was simply focussed on the king in particular. It was in token of this that the king was regarded as a consecrated person, and this was marked by the ceremony of anointing – he was a 'messiah'.

This too explains some of the very bold language

used of the king. He is even, for example, called a divine being: 'Your throne, God, will last for ever and ever' (Ps 45:6): 'His name will be Mighty God, Father Eternal, Prince of Peace' (Is 9:5). The traditional figure for Israel's God, 'the shepherd', was applied to the king: 'I mean to raise up one shepherd, my servant David' (Ez 34:21). Israel's privileged position of divine sonship – 'Israel is my first-born son' (Ex 4:22) – was applied to the king: 'Thou art my son, this day I have begotton thee' (Ps 2:7).

As time went on, successive kings of Israel failed utterly to live up to the national ideals, failed utterly to bring their hopes nearer to realisation. So Israel's hopes reached forward to a new David, an ideal king, a perfect messiah. So that when the new testament says 'Jesus is the Christ', they are saying that he is the ideal king of Israel's hopes, the one who would bring prosperity and victory, but who would also bring to perfection the covenant relationship, that bond between God and the people, and restore justice, unity and peace.

But even this was not the whole story. For to say that Israel was God's chosen people is not to say that the rest of mankind was rejected. On the contrary, Israel's privileged position was for the sake of others; they were to be 'a priestly people', bringing the world's worship to God and God's blessing to the world. The Spirit of God was not for them alone but was to be poured out on all mankind (Jl 3:1); all nations would seek God's will which was enshrined in Israel's law (Is 2:2-3); their father Abraham was promised a blessing not only for his descendants but for all the nations of the world (Gen 12:3). This idea underlies the bible's account of 'pre-history' in the early chapters of Genesis – even here, before attention is focussed on Israel in particular, God is at work amongst men; right back to the origins of mankind, where God promises that some day, somehow, some son of woman would undo the harm that is in the world (Gen 3:15).

In other words, when we talk about the covenant with Israel we are really talking about God's love for all men, focussed on Israel; and when we talk about 'the messiah', we are talking about this covenant as it is focussed on the person of Israel's hoped-for king. So, to say that Jesus is the Christ, the messiah, means more than that he is the great king Israel hoped for; it even means much more than that he is the fulfilment of Israel's hopes and ideals expressed in the covenant; it means that he is the fulfilment of the hopes and ideals of the whole of mankind. Through him, the world's despair is overcome; on him our lives depend. In him, we are given the hope and promise that we too can be sons of God: 'God became man in order that men may become gods'. 'O little town of Bethlehem', we sing in one of the Christmas carols, 'The hopes and fears of all the years are found in you today'.

The man for all men

But here, at the end of this glance at the new testament ways of presenting Jesus to us, a point of some theological importance emerges. It is really a repetition of a point already made (p 2f) – that religion is not synonymous with theology; that the point of our religion is not information about God, not clear understanding of profound truths, but a personal relationship between God and ourselves. It is a truism to say that a man may be a great theologian without being particularly holy; and the reverse is also true – that a person may be in a very close relationship with God without being able to put it into words. And it is obviously the latter that is important: our relationship with God, not our ability to discuss it. Similarly, then, it is not the point of the bible to provide information, abstract knowledge or deep philosophical ideas. What our Lord came to

31

do was 'to give us life and give it more abundantly' (Jn 10:10). (It is true that he also says 'This is eternal life, to know thee, the one true God . . .'; but the word 'know' in the language of the bible means a living knowledge which comes from the possession of life). What the new testament is trying to do is not to discuss theoretical ideas but to make available to us this life: 'These things are written in order that you may believe, and believing, have life in his name' (Jn 20:31).

And this too is surely the task of the christian teacher. Obviously we must strive for clarity and accuracy, and certainly we must try not to give the wrong idea; but what we are really trying to do is to make available the reality of the life given to us by our Lord.

And the end of our consideration of Jesus, the Christ, suggests a possible approach to this. We have seen that what we really mean when we say that Jesus is the messiah is that he is the one who brings to fulfilment the hopes and ideals of all mankind. A possible catechesis, therefore, might go like this. One might begin by starting a discussion of people who have influenced us (obviously I am thinking of senior pupils) – parents, elder brothers and sisters, teachers . . . Then we might broaden this into a discussion of people who have influenced the world, who have made a difference to the way we live: Lenin, Freud, Picasso, Baird, the inventor of television, Bell, the inventor of the telephone . . . especially people from the more remote past: Shakespeare, William the Conqueror, Napoleon, the unknown inventor of the alphabet, Luther . . . And after we have discussed this thoroughly, seen how and what influence they have had, then one might conclude something like this: 'There is another person who lived two thousand years ago, who wasn't really famous in the same way as some of them – he came from a working class family in a small village in a poor country in the Middle East; the Roman emperor who ruled the country had never heard of him; he wasn't rich; he never wrote a book; he wasn't even particularly successful – his own people executed him as a criminal. He didn't found a political party, he didn't conquer any lands, he didn't invent anything. But what he did was to make it possible for everybody, for us today, to live a life like God's.

In doing this we haven't proved anything; what we have done is expound the christian faith, we have shown why Christ is important. Above all we haven't proved that he was God. But if we have given an accurate, abstract definition and explanation of the hypostatic union, but haven't said why it is important to us, have we really done anything worth while? Whereas if we can convey the overwhelming importance of what Jesus has done, of what Jesus alone can do, then have we not really come very close to the heart of the mystery of Jesus, true God and true man?

Note
(1) To say that the gospels prove that our Lord was God is not so much false as a wrong way of putting it, both as far as the gospels themselves are concerned and for us. They are not proving anything; they are presenting our Lord to us, and proclaiming him. We can, if we care to do so, use the gospels to prove something, just as we can use Boswell's *Life of Johnson* to prove something about Dr Johnson; but this is not why they were written, not as text books for apologetics. They present him to us; and they present him in a way which will try to take proper account of the extraordinary paradoxical facets of his character and yet make sense. Not that we have any doubt about the divinity of our Lord;

we accept gladly and confidently the formulae of the ancient creeds and councils – that Jesus is the only Son of God, consubstantial with the Father, a divine and human nature bound in a hypostatic union. Only it may be doubted whether many non-theologians find this a particularly helpful way to think realistically about Jesus; and above all we may doubt whether this is what the new testament is trying to say to us. Following the new testament, it seems more useful to try to find some insight into the mystery of the person of Jesus – this mystery which the later theologians expressed in their own language.

4

Redemption

Any christian can tell you what our Lord did. He saved us, he redeemed us. He died for us. He died to save us from sin. And if we asked how his death saved us, we would probably get this sort of answer: all of us were born in a state of sin, a state of enmity with God, and the cruel death of God's beloved Son appeased his anger and reconciled us to him. And this is where the trouble starts.

But before we start trying to cope with the trouble, let us clear up two preliminary points. First, can we leave the question of sin out of this for the moment? It is true that no matter how you explain the redemption sin has something to do with it; but what I am going to suggest is that it doesn't have everything to do with it; and our consideration of the redemption is liable to be confused and bedevilled by this important, but additional, point.

Secondly, here once more the consideration applies that we have made often enough already – that what we mean by revelation is not information but an act, something God does, an approach he makes to us, a relationship he enters into. The fact comes first, and the attempt to formulate the fact, to describe it, to understand it, comes at a later stage; and the latter is not necessarily synonymous with the former. Our attempts at formulating what God has done are not necessarily complete and exhaustive descriptions of the fact, so that sometimes several different ways of looking at it are necessary to bring out different aspects of the truth. This was true in the old testament; they looked at their relationship with God from several points of view and therefore expressed their hopes in several different ways; and christians, who saw in their own experience the fulfilment of the old testament hopes, adopted these various formulae. The Israelites described the close bond between themselves and God as a covenant, and therefore looked forward to a new covenant (Jer 31:31). They saw in their possession of the land flowing with milk and honey a sign of God's loving care for them, and they looked for an even richer, more prosperous life. The king was God's representative for them, making Israel the beginning of God's kingdom in the world, and they looked forward to an ideal king who would bring God's kingdom to perfection. They recognised that God's life was in them – he breathed into the face of man who became a living spirit; they recognised too that this life-giving power came strikingly close to certain individuals such as judges and prophets; and they looked forward to the day when the same dynamic possession of the Spirit would be the possession of all men (Jl 3:1).

When our Lord came, then, it was from all these different points of view that christians were able to look at his work. He came to make a new covenant between God and man; he came to renew the face of the earth; he came to found the kingdom of God; he came to send the Spirit. Therefore, when we so briefly describe our Lord's work as 'redemption' and define this as liberation from sin, let us recognise that this is an almost breathtakingly laconic and summary way of describing a much richer reality.

And when it comes to describing *how* our Lord carried out his work, the means by which he achieved it, the same principle holds. All that we have in the first place is the fact. We used to say – we still do – that he died to redeem us; nowadays we realise that his death without the resurrection would be incomplete, so we know that what we really mean is that he redeemed us by his death and resurrection. But even this is something of an abbreviation. Some texts of the new testament and some of the fathers of the church put a great deal of stress on the incarnation – the mere fact of God becoming man transformed the human situation. And on the other hand, can we really leave out the ascension, or the sending of the Spirit? Surely these too are elements in our Lord's redeeming work.

However, at least as an abbreviation let us accept that his death and resurrection are the heart of the matter. But when we say this we have merely stated the fact; we have not yet said exactly how his death and resurrection achieved what God wanted. And one difficulty about the word 'redemption' is that besides describing the work of Christ it also implies a theory about the way in which he achieved it. The derivation of the word (ultimately from the Latin *emere*, meaning 'to buy') suggests that it was a 'buying back' – with all that such an interpretation implies; that we were slaves, and that our Lord's death was the price paid for our freedom. I am not at the moment concerned to argue for or against such an interpretation[1]. What is important to realise is that it *is* an interpretation, one theory amongst others. Indeed, the work of Christ is so full of meaning that it seems impossible to find any one way of describing it which will do full justice to the reality; and that is why the new testament does not present us with *a* theology – one single, consistent, watertight definition – but with various ways of looking at it which will bring out various facets of the truth.

What I would like to do here is to present just three of these different ways of looking at it; not of course contradictory or mutually exclusive, to a certain extent overlapping one with the other, each one to a certain extent incomplete by itself. But first of all they will illustrate the fact that there are various ways of looking at Christ's work; and secondly, this may help us to feel free to think about it now in one way and now in another, depending on the context.

The passover

The simplest and in many ways the most satisfactory way of looking at it consists simply in describing the facts. He died, and he rose again. He 'passed out of this world to the Father' (Jn 13:1) and this transition was a transformation of the human situation. It was the first time any member of the human race had done this, but it started a fashion, so to speak – it opened up possibilities: he is the first; but not the last, he is 'the first-born of many brethren' (Rom 8:29, cf 1 Cor 15:23). It is a 'passover' and can be visualised on the analogy of the exodus from Egypt (and in the account of the transfiguration this is exactly what one of the gospels calls our Lord's death: 'Moses and Elijah appeared with him, talking about his *exodus*, his death' Lk 9:31) – it is a transition from slavery to freedom, from darkness to light, from death to life. He shared our life to the full, our sufferings, our sorrows; now, by dying, he puts an end to that sort of life and starts another, a new life, a glorious, triumphant life, a life to God, a life with God: St Paul compares it to a woman who, according to the Roman law, was under the rule of her husband; but of course this lasts only as long as the husband is alive – once he dies the woman is freed (Rom 7:1-3). 'Christ having died will die no more, death has no more power over him. When he died, he died once for all, his life now is life with God' (Rom 6:8-10).

38

A gift of love

Although this way of looking at it is in many ways the most satisfactory, it has one evident weakness – it treats the death of our Lord almost casually, almost as a mere prelude to the resurrection. It would not make much difference to this way of putting it if our Lord had died peacefully in his bed. So another train of thought (one which we find particularly in St John's gospel) pays more attention to the death, particularly to the suffering it involved. But not just as suffering, as mere pain. We might begin with the words: 'God so loved the world as to give his Son . . .' (Jn 3:16). The whole of religion is based on God giving us himself – not on revelation in the sense of giving us information, not on commands issued from above; but on God coming to us, making himself available to us, in Jesus his Son. And then Jesus in his turn continues the process – he too shows his love for men, and shows it in giving: 'Having loved his own who were in the world he loved them to the end' (Jn 13:1); to the end – not just to the last moment but to the last degree, to the utmost; by giving everything he had, his life, his last breath and his last drop of blood. The death of Jesus, then, is in the fullest sense of the word a love token. But it is not simply a token. It is a real gift of himself that he gives. He gives his life not only for us, but to us. One way of putting it – a figurative way, but it is an expressive figure – is suggested by the fourth gospel; when our Lord died, John says: 'He breathed forth his spirit'; obviously at one level a metaphorical expression for 'he breathed his last', 'he gave up the ghost'. But the deeper meaning of the metaphor is brought out by a passage almost immediately after this where the risen Lord breathes on his disciples and says, 'Receive the Holy Spirit'. The life our Lord gives up is the life he gives to us, the divine life, the Spirit of God.

With urgent love, Jesus gives us everything he has, gives us his life, offers it to us. All we have to do is accept this gift, to open our hearts and receive it. This is what we call redemption.

An act of repentance

This last way of looking at it pays due attention to Christ's death, more than the first way did. But even so it does not take sufficient account of the suffering it involved, the agony and pain and humiliation of our human condition embraced by Christ. Here above all one cannot avoid bringing in the question of sin, which as we have said is reserved for fuller consideration later. But even without any further consideration no one would deny that our human situation is one of alienation from God. Now it may indeed be argued that a created human being even at its best could not have achieved union with God without the action and life of God made man. But that action and life had to take a particular form because of the sinful situation of mankind.

Still trying to avoid going too deeply into the question of sin, we may say that it is essentially a wrong choice, a selfish choice, a choice of ourselves rather than of God; and it means that we have a tendency to make that sort of choice, that our bent is inwards rather than outwards and upwards. And human suffering is – not exactly a punishment from God – but a sign of our alienation from God. God is all good; and our wrong choice is the rejection of this good. If a mother tells her child to keep away from an electric hot-plate, the child touches it and gets its fingers burnt, this is not a punishment, it is just the result; but it is the result of doing what it shouldn't do, and the pain is also a message that the child has done wrong and that the mother was right. And Christ's suffering is his sharing in the human suffering which is the sign of our having strayed from God; but in him, it is a counter-choice, a choice of God, and more specifically it is a choice of God at the expense of himself. In him, suffering becomes a recognition and acceptance of the fact that we have gone wrong, and therefore that God is right. It may be called an act of repentance – a *metanoia* – a change of mind and a change of heart expressed in the very suffering which is the mark of our wrongfulness. Suppose we are taking one of those short cuts which eventually leave us completely lost; the first thing to do is to recognise that we are lost – otherwise we may go on further and further in the wrong direction. But to recognise that we are lost is the first step to finding our way back to the right road. And this is what Christ has done. 'He who was sinless became sin for us' (2 Cor 5:21); he identified himself with our human situation with all its sufferings. But what in us is the pathetic passive mark of our misery, in him – in his heart, in his body – becomes a joyful, loving, adoring acclamation of God who is good; who alone is good; outside of whom there is only misery and darkness.

And of course God is there, unchanging love, to receive this return to himself. To say that God is angry with us can be a misleading figure of speech, especially to children. It is traditional and biblical language, and it does very powerfully express a certain truth, the hatefulness of sin. But it does not mean that God ever turns away from us. God *is* love; he not only happens to love us or decides to love us; he is love, and he can no more cease to love us than he can cease to be God. Our separation from God is a one-sided affair; we can turn away from him, but he cannot turn away from us; and as soon as we turn back to him, he is there with open arms to receive us.

Christ as our representative has shown us the way

back to God. This is what one of the prophets hoped for in words that have always been applied to our Lord: 'All we like sheep had gone astray; but he bore our sorrows, he carried our sufferings; and by his wounds, we were healed' (Is 53:4-6). Suffering and death, the very sign of our separation from God, is now in him a sign of turning back to God.

By baptism we share in this work of Christ, 'we are baptised into his death' (Rom 6:3). It makes available to us his return to God, his love expressed in suffering and death; but it is a pledge too that we will make our sufferings and death in union with his an act of loving return to our Father.

Note:

(1) Though many theologians today would say that of all the possible ways of talking about the work of Christ, this is the least satisfactory. To mention only one difficulty, it seems to leave the resurrection almost entirely out of the picture; yet it is obviously essential; cf Peter de Rosa, *God our Saviour*, p 80; F.X. Durrwell, *The Resurrection*, pp 28-31).

5

Sin and sinfulness

We all know what sin is: sin is a deliberate offence against God. This sounds clear and simple enough; but like many a simple, clear formula it conceals a great deal of complexity. For example, what is meant by 'offence'? Many people would probably say that it is a transgression of God's command. But even this is not absolutely clear; does it mean that all sins are essentially disobedience? and does it mean that God gives commands simply to test our obedience (like the mother who says, 'See what Tommy's doing and tell him to stop')?

But the main point we have to make clear to ourselves is that our idea of sin is intrinsically connected with our idea of God. For example, in some pagan religions the gods were mysteriously present in certain areas of human life and even in certain objects or places; and 'sin' was anything which trespassed on these areas even unknowingly; if the stream was sacred to the god then to tamper with its waters was a 'sin' and was followed by punishment (though in practice of course it was usually the other way about – the person suffered some misfortune and in order to explain it he tried to find out what god he had offended, and how). Similarly, if we regard God as a tyrant intent merely on asserting his supremacy and our subjection, then sin will be any transgression of his edict; or to put it the other way round, if you regard sin as primarily the transgression of an edict, it implies that your idea of God is one who demands above all obedience.

So to understand sin, we have to go back to our idea of God as we have already considered it. God is a person, a personal being, with intelligence and will; not impersonal power, but one who acts meaningfully. His will, moreover, is 'good will': quite simply – as simply as the new testament – we can say God is love.

This love expresses itself in outgoing action, in creation. And here we may pause a moment. If this is really our view of God and of creation, then any imperfection in creation cannot be treated lightly; it is wrong. The bible would find no difficulty in using the word 'sin' of this situation; and although it might only lead to confusion for us to use it in this way – to use the word sin for cancer or famine, for example – nevertheless we should recognise that the two areas of material and spiritual wrongness cannot simply be separated.

But we recognise God's love especially in relation to ourselves; he comes out to men, comes to them offering them the capacity to live at something like his level of existence, with the capacity to love, to share, to communicate: with above all the capacity to be free, with the freedom to be and the freedom to grow. And again we may pause, if only to realise how far we have come from the idea of a God who simply issues commands. God wants us to be free. If we asked ourselves, 'Does God want us to be good, or does he want us to be free?', we would probably try to evade the question by saying that he wants both. But if we pressed the question, if only to clarify the issue, does he want free human beings or does he want automata who mechanically follow a set pattern of action, no matter how virtuous and worthy; then undoubtedly our answer would be the former – he wants us to be free.

This is what God wants. And we are *not* like that.

44

We do not love enough, we don't even know how to love; we cannot communicate; we are not free; we are either inhibited or (and) eccentric, unbalanced; we are bound and limited, by our circumstances, by an inadequate control of our environment, by inability to cooperate with other people, but even more – even if these disabilities were overcome – we are limited by ourselves, our own pettyness, our own selfishness, our own lack of understanding, our own narrowness.

We are like this. We all realise it, and literature is full of it. Perhaps the most graphic description of the human situation is given by St Paul: 'I cannot understand my own behaviour. I fail to carry out the things I want to do, and I find myself doing the very things I hate. The will to do what is good is in me, the performance is not, with the result that instead of doing the good things I want to do, I carry out the sinful things I do not want. This seems to be the rule, that every single time I want to do something good, it is something evil that comes to hand. In my inmost self I dearly love God's law, but I can see that my body follows a different law that battles against the law that my reason dictates' (Rom 7:14-23). We are like this. But why? And again literature is full of variations on the question, and variations of answers.

Original sin

The traditional christian answer is often expressed in the doctrine of original sin. This goes roughly like this: that the first human couple were created with none of the disabilities familiar to us, but through a deliberate transgression of God's command, a deliberate rejection of God's will for them, they lost both for themselves and for their descendants – the whole human race – this state of innocence and incurred this distortion of the human situation in which we live.

45

This is a deep-rooted christian tradition (so deep that, as we shall say in a moment, we cannot simply ignore it); but it all goes back to the narrative at the beginning of Genesis. There are several difficulties about the interpretation of the passage – none of them fatal, none of them that christian scholars have not already considered and found an answer to. But there is one particular difficulty which should make us pause; and that is that as an explanation, it raises almost as many problems as it solves. It is important to remember that what we are concerned with, and what the author of Genesis was concerned with, is not simply the moral inadequacy of the human race, but the total wrong situation in which we find ourselves. If God is good – and that must be our starting point – then any fault in the world which he has made must be unacceptable. Storms, droughts, earthquakes, violence, the pain and suffering of the animal world – these too are 'wrong', as St Paul recognises when he speaks of 'creation unable to attain its purpose; from the beginning till now the whole creation has been groaning' (Rom 8:20-22). And how does the sin of the first human beings apply to this situation? It was easier for the author of Genesis who thought of man as being present in the world practically from the beginning; but now that we know that man is a relative newcomer in creation, that for thousands of millions of years before the first man appeared the world had been going on, and going on with the same imperfections as we know today, then it is not so easy to see how man's sin can be responsible for those imperfections.

So we seem to be back where we started, with a problem to which there is no answer. What do we do now? One thing we cannot do is simply to ignore and reject the teaching of the bible and the christian tradition. Christian tradition is not like that, as we shall see later (p 65f) – a random accumulation of out-dated opinions. Some elements of this tradition – and this appears to be one of them – enter so deeply into our christian being that (as with certain experiences in our individual lives) to reject them would be a traumatic experience. And even if we did reject this solution, the problem would still remain, the facts would still be there – a world disfigured by imperfections, alienation, inhibition, sin.

What we can do, what we must do, is to look at the problem again and see if we can find some way of looking at it which will remain true to the fundamental insight offered to us by the author of Genesis, but which will not be false either to other data, particularly those offered to us by the scientists. In other words, can we restate Genesis in a way which would be acceptable to the author if he were writing today?

What we are offering, then, is a hypothesis. And the key to the hypothesis, as it is the key to the problem, is this question of imperfection (for as we have seen, it is not merely a matter of moral weakness in men, but of a whole world which is imperfect, and of the connexion between the two). It may help us to clarify the situation if we consider two examples. Take a child of a few months, and a very old man. These are both 'imperfect' human beings, with much the same kind of imperfections: they don't see very clearly, they don't speak very clearly, they don't walk very well, they can't feed themselves properly, they can't co-ordinate, and so on. Both imperfect human beings, with much the same kind of disability. And yet we are all clearly aware that the word 'imperfection', though correctly used of both of them, means something very different in each; the one is the imperfection of growth, of potentiality, and will lead to maturity; the other is the imperfection of decrepitude and will end with death.

But this puts our original difficulty into an entirely

new light. Could God make an imperfect world? Our first reaction is to say no; but now we realise that the question conceals an ambiguity and needs to be re-stated like this: could God make an imperfect world? imperfect in the sense of the second of our examples, imperfect with the imperfection of an old man tottering on the brink of extinction, with a radical, intrinsic, irreparable imperfection – then the answer is no. But could God make the world imperfect in the other sense, with the imperfection of growth and potentiality? Then the answer is yes; indeed, if we accept the view of the world held almost unconsciously by virtually everyone today, an evolutionary view, then we are saying not only that God could do this, but that this is in fact what he has done. To accept evolution is to accept the fact that God did not produce a ready-made cosmos, not one that was 'perfect'; that creation is not a static act but a dynamic process, in which there is development, growth, potentiality.

It is on this basis, then, that we can proceed with our hypothesis. In the course of this development, living beings emerge, beings with the ability to react to their environment. The mechanism for doing this was the nervous system, and eventually a species emerges with a highly developed nervous system, with the capacity to assimilate and store various different factors in its environment, and to evaluate them; to this class, Man belongs. Whether certain non-human species also share this capacity; or again, whether the present human species is one of a wider group to which the label *Homo* could be given – these are questions which for our present purposes need not concern us. What I mean by man in the present context is a being with the ability to choose. He is not merely part of nature, but is also in some sense outside it; he is both a product of the evolutionary process and yet also its master – he can control the process of evolution.

To return now to a more directly theological view-point, man is faced with a choice; to be a man is to be faced with a choice. In modern terms one might say that it is a choice between collaborating with God in the making of the world, or to distort the world to his own personal end. But this is to put it in modern terms, and it is not necessary to imagine that the first human beings would have a very clear and explicit idea either of the nature of God or of the nature of the choice. But to be a man at all, in the sense that we are postulating here, is to be aware of the fact that he is not simply at the mercy of blind forces, that he can to some extent control his environment; and this control can be exercised in a positive way, that will contribute to the harmonious development of his world, or it can be exercised in a negative way which will distort it. And man in fact chooses the latter – with the disas-trous consequences we know. Not that the world was perfect before this, but its imperfection was one of potentiality; it is through man's intervention that the development takes the form of a distortion. And this distortion marks the world in which we live – we all contribute to it, it affects our attitude to everything in life, it affects our bodies, our minds, it is a deficiency handed on with other psychological characteristics by heredity. [1]

Sinfulness

This is the human situation. Into this situation, Christ enters. 'He came to save us from our sins', we say; and it could sound like a comic-strip hero swooping down to defeat the villain and then sweeping out again. But Christ did more than that. Christ enters our human situation, a situation marred by selfishness, bitterness, pettyness and frustration. He accepts this situation, he identifies himself with it. But where all other men fail,

he uniquely succeeded. Not that he completely transformed the world in which we live (this complete
transformation, 'a new heaven and a new earth', does
indeed come within his total work, though it is something we still wait for). He did not even explain the
imperfections of our world. And it should perhaps be
noted that we too have not really attempted to explain
it. We have not tried to explain *why* our world should
be so imperfect, why our wills so habitually veer
towards evil rather than towards good. What we have
suggested is a way of looking at it which fits in with our
normal way of looking at the world today, but we have
not claimed to solve the mystery of evil. We are no
worse off than anyone else in this; this is an enigma
which the greatest minds have always recognised, but
it still remains an enigma. We are no worse off, but
neither are we any better off. Christianity does not
claim to have theoretical answers to theoretical questions. What it does offer – what Christ offers – is a
practical answer: how best to live within the world we
have. This Christ did. In a life like ours, he was fully
free; neither environment nor heredity nor convention
were able to warp or cramp him.

He did this, and made it possible for us to live a life
like his (see above, p 32f). We are born into a world
already marred by fear and ignorance, already in-
fected by selfishness and pettyness and dishonesty and
lovelessness. We breathe this atmosphere, it stunts and
cripples us. And now, in place of this, Christ has provided an atmosphere, an environment, where real
communication is possible, a free and loving exchange
and a mutually enriching giving. Into this new environment the christian enters by baptism, into the body
of Christ.

But like birth, this is a beginning, not an end. The
call of God in Christ is a call to freedom; not to the
mechanical performance of right actions. To be reborn

in Christ is not to be magically transformed into an angelic being; it is to be given a new source of life, and the possibility and the means to live it. The persons who are called to live this life are still persons subject to the disabilities of our heredity and environment, still therefore subject to sin. But for a christian, this is what sin is; it is the failure to live out the implications of our baptism, this pledge to live and grow in freedom and love after the standard of Christ and in union with him.

This is the measure and the standard of sinfulness. We, with our total human personality, have been inserted into the victorious human life, the divine life, which is in Christ; and sin is a failure to live that life. It is not a matter of individual actions, but of our whole personality. It is true that our personality is reflected in individual actions, but how much of our full personality is involved in any individual act is often difficult to say. This is what makes the judgment of sin and guilt a difficult process. But certainly it cannot be judged solely by measuring an individual act against the yardstick of law. If we judge by law, we are in danger of accusing ourselves of things in which our personality may be only very slightly involved; and equally, of failing to criticise those factors in our personality which are real failures by the standard of Christ. 'I am not conscious of anything in myself, but this does not mean that I am justified; the Lord alone is my judge' (1 Cor 4:4).

This is the criterion. And by this criterion we all fail, almost all the time, by comparison with the unutterable beauty and nobility of the person of Christ. We fail. But there is nothing here for either despair or presumption, if our efforts are directed, not simply to trying to live good lives, but to fit ourselves into the transforming power of the Spirit of God in Christ.

51

(1) Why did man make this choice? This is the limit of explanation even in a hypothesis such as the one we are elaborating. To be a man is to have a real capacity for choice, and to ask why he should make one choice rather than another is simply to ask the question, 'Why is a man?'

6

The church

The church: this is what modern jargon would call 'an emotive term', to judge by the wide range of response the word evokes. A society which will oppose anything that most people favour; an institution which goes in for quaint ritual; gentlemen in black with ill-defined occupations; why don't 'the churches' stop playing about with rubrics and dogmas and do something about the state of the world. Amongst catholics, the word is very often used as if it were synonymous with a particular group; people say 'the church' when they are really referring to the pope, or his officials or the bishops or clergy or religious. And then there are a number of traditional clichés associated with the word: the one ark of salvation, the source of infallible truth, the unchanging bulwark against falsehood and error, supreme fount of holiness, 'Holy Mother Church'. It is this last which probably causes greatest confusion; for no normal person, certainly no normal christian, can think of himself as 'holy' – and therefore he tends to project 'churchness' onto others, nuns and priests and so on, with the resulting distinction between 'them' and 'us'.

This attitude – or rather this complex of attitudes, not really synthesised – is already changing. One of the factors in the change is the return to the bible; a comparison with the people of God as it exists there makes it clear how much of the present situation is not biblical, how much it owes to medieval juridical and political structures. Another factor in the changing attitude is the ecumenical movement which is forcing us to think again about the real nature of the church, what constitutes membership of it, what it is for. But for catholics this change of attitude results in yet further confusion: if the Roman catholic church is the one true church, then what about other christian bodies? If it isn't, then what is all the fuss about? If the church is the one ark of salvation, then what about those who are not members of it? If it isn't, then what is the point of it? It is to these multiple confusions that we are addressing ourselves here.

Organisation or person?

The most obvious thing about the church (at first sight) is that it is some sort of society. One may begin, therefore, by thinking of other societies we know, in order to bring out what is specific to this one. Is it like a trade union? like a political party? like a sports club? like a charitable organisation, like Oxfam? like a society for the propagation of the gospel?

But the main difference between the church and any of these is that the church is not devoted to limited purposes or sectional interests. It is a society in the same sense as the human race is a society; in principle at least, it is co-extensive with the human race. It is for all men in the same way as Christ is for all men.

But this reference to Christ gives us another possible blue-print of a society by which to measure the church. Is it 'a society of Christ' in the same way as you might have a Shakespearian society, or a Winston Churchill society? Is it a society founded by Christ and dedicated to fostering the ideals of its founder? It is; and this might be a good way to understand the church, provided we remember what his ideals were.

Christ, as we have seen, involved himself totally in the human situation, and transcended it by his death and resurrection. He did this not only in himself but as the representative of the human race. His achievement did not produce an automatic change in the human situation, but took the form of an offer – necessarily so, since his work is a work of liberation, of freedom; if he gives us freedom he cannot impose it on us. He offers us freedom – freedom to be, freedom to grow, freedom to love.

But it is not only this ideal that he offered us. He offered us his own life; he sent us his Spirit; and 'to those who received him, he gave power to be sons of God' (Jn 1:12). Those who accepted his offer have a new life; they are a breakthrough in human existence; they form a 'new creation'. They form a new type of society – this new life does not belong to each of them individually, it is essentially something they have in common. So they try to find ways of describing this new type of society.

They call themselves a new people, a new 'nation'; because they are not unlike the socio-political associations in which men live, only now this is a new one; you have Romans and Germans and Hibernians and Athenians – and now christians; a new people, which however does not conflict with any of the others but transcends them. In particular the word 'nation' attracts them, because it is from the Latin word meaning 'to be born', and this group forms a *natio* by being 'reborn'.

But this then suggests another and even stronger metaphor – this group of people is like a family. For the ties that bind them together, which make them what they are, are not merely the cultural, historical or geographical ties of a nation, but the real bond of life and common birth which constitutes a family.

But even the family relationship does not do full

justice to this new society, and especially to its relationship with Christ. A child's life begins in its mother's womb, formed entirely by elements contributed by both parents, and once born it lives and grows in the love and care of the parents; but as it grows, it grows increasingly *away* from its parents – and this is right, this is the goal of true parental love, to enable the child to exist and grow as an independent person. But those who are reborn in Christ are not only born of God but live with the power of life continually drawn from him, the Spirit of God; and growth for them is not growth away from their source, but growth into God. Each of them is an independent person, each is different, with different characteristics and gifts; but the goal, the ideal, is 'to grow into perfect manhood according to the stature of Christ' (Eph 4:13), and their different gifts are to contribute to this completeness. So, for this new society, another and more vivid comparison comes to mind: it is like a *body* – the body of Christ.

There are three different implications in this metaphor of the body. First of all it points to the unity which binds the group together, a unity greater than that of a nation or a family; a unity, moreover, which is not simply uniformity. For a body, a human body, is not like a stone or a block of wood; it is made up of many different parts all working harmoniously together. And it is the same in this society formed by Christ; each individual retains his individuality, his own character, his own outlook, but all of these contribute to the total good of the whole community. 'If the foot were to say, I am not the hand and so I do not belong to the body, would that mean that it stopped being part of the body? If the ear were to say, I am not the eye and so I do not belong to the body, would that mean that it was not a part of the body? If your whole body was just one eye, how would you hear anything?

If it was just one ear, how would you smell anything? As it is, the parts are many but the body is one. Now you together are Christ's body . . .' (1 Cor 12:12–30).

A body is a unity composed of different members all working together. It is not a single, undifferentiated mass, nor on the other hand is it a random collection of completely different elements. Its unity springs from a common vital principle. And this is the second implication of the metaphor 'body' applied to the church. It is the body *of Christ*. He is the vital principle which gives unity to the whole body. 'He is the head by whom the whole body is fitted and joined together, each joint adding its own strength for each separate part to work according to its function' (Eph 4:16). The biology is not particularly accurate, and of course the metaphor must not be pressed too far, but the idea is clear enough; the church is a living organism forming one being with Christ himself.

And this leads us to the third implication of the metaphor. A body is something visible, material. It is not a ghost, not a spirit. Our Lord was a bodily person in this sense when he lived on earth. But after his death and resurrection, although he was still – is still – a real person, he no longer moves amongst us in the same visible tangible way. And this is the function of 'the body of Christ'; this body, this society of human beings sharing the life of Christ, is visible and plays the same part in the world now as Christ played when he himself was on earth. If you like (and remembering that we are dealing in figures of speech), we now have a body, a single organic whole, whose head is invisible and whose body is visible.

The role of the body

This makes us better able to understand the purpose and function of the church; but in order to deal with this, we have to go back on our steps a moment and ask again what Christ's purpose and function was; for if the church is his body, it exists to continue his work. He came to redeem the world, to remake, reform the human situation, to transform it into something divine. One formula used to describe this is to say that Christ came to found 'the kingdom of God' – a world restored, a world made perfect, a world in which God will be all in all (1 Cor 15:28, cf Col 1:19, Eph 1:23).

If then we ask if Christ came to found the church, the answer is no – not primarily, not in the first place. His work is much wider than this, and the church plays a part in this wider role. It exists to carry out Christ's redeeming work. It is not an end in itself; it is a means to an end.

But it is not as simple as this. The church performs its task not merely as a group of people who have dedicated themselves to carrying on their master's ideal (as a communist might claim to be a marxist or a leninist), nor even as a society commissioned and accredited to do so (though they are this too – they are 'apostles'). The church performs its task not merely in memory of its founder, not merely with his authority, but in virtue of this vital union with Christ which is the church's being. The church acts through Christ, with Christ and in Christ. It is the body of Christ, living with a life that comes from him in order to act visibly amongst men on his behalf, with his power, in his name. The church is indeed the community of those who are redeemed; but it is not simply the cosy coterie of the elect. It is redeemed, in order to carry on the work of redeeming.

So if we now ask again the question, did Christ come to found a church, the answer would be yes; but not to be an end in itself. It is a sample of what the world should be, the first fruits. It is a prototype of a redeemed, reconciled, liberated, sanctified community. Let us take an example. Suppose you wanted to make a bonfire, and you gathered together the paper and sticks and bits of wood. You would then strike a match. But as soon as you strike the match you already have a fire – a small fire, a 'prototype'. You then apply the burning match to your bundle of paper and sticks to spread this small fire to the bigger one. But you wouldn't get a blaze at all unless you started with the small fire of the match; and equally the burning match is not the end of the matter – you don't strike the match and say, 'Good, now we've got the fire', and forget all about your heap of wood there; the burning match exists in order to light the heap. In the same way, the church exists to bring redemption to the world, but it does so by being itself redeemed.

The church is the first-fruits of a redeemed community. This is why we can – we do, inevitably – speak of the church as something different from ourselves. Although we belong to it, although it is made up of people like ourselves, nevertheless the church is not simply us, it is not simply the sum total of its visible members. We do not perfectly embody the perfection of the church – this fully redeemed and redeeming community, the body of Christ, holy, joyful, free. There are elements in us, aspects of our nature, which are not fully redeemed, and which to this extent are not completely integrated with our status as members of the church. The church, understood in this way, is never a completely realised ideal; it is always in a state of becoming. It is not a single, disruptive reformation that the church needs, but a continual process of reformation, a continual process of striving to be more perfectly the ideal church. And yet the ideal church is not merely an abstraction. It is a reality; there are people who do perfectly embody the ideal. We are quite right to make the distinction between 'them' and 'us' which we referred to earlier, but we pick on the wrong 'them'. The failure to be perfectly integrated into the ideal affects every living member of the church – popes, bishops, priests, nuns, as well as the most unruly primary school child. The ideal church is Christ himself, the head, and the community of those who have finally achieved complete union with him. 'We are part of a building that has the apostles and prophets for its foundation, and Christ Jesus himself for its chief cornerstone' (Eph 2:20). And above all it is true of Mary, the only human being who during her life time perfectly embodied the ideal – born without sin, fully redeemed, empty and full of grace, stripped of the distortions that mar the rest of us, growing and flowering in beauty and nobility, bringing forth God into the world.

The divided church

God's will for the world is something greater than the church; or at least greater than the church which we know and belong to. The church exists to be a prototype of a harmonious, integrated world. And this is the scandal of a divided church of Christ, and this is what lies behind our quest for unity. It is not a question of a merger, like a business, to produce a more massive organisation with more impressive numbers. It is because a divided church is a contradiction in terms. The church exists to be the sign, the beacon of a world made one; and how tragic it is when it fails in this task, and mirrors in its very being the divisions it exists to heal.

The quest for unity takes the form of a search to find what aspects of the church are verified in any human situation; or, putting it the other way round, the church tries to find what elements in the human ideal can be embraced and fostered by her as elements of her own true nature. Thus we can share with the Hindu, for example, the deep respect for all forms of life as embodying something of the divine. We can respect and share that unyielding faith in one God which is characteristic of the mohammedan religion. We can appreciate and foster the ideal of a people of God which we share with the Jews. The search for unity is not an attempt at conquest, nor is it a process of bargaining and negotiation and compromise. It does not consist of a denial of any truth which we ourselves hold, but in an affirmation of the good we see in others.

Among those who claim the title of fellow-christians the same principle holds, but the relationship is obviously much closer. With our fellow-christians of different denominations we recognise the many bonds that spring from our common following of Christ – the ideal of his life, the authority of his teaching, the power of the scriptures which bear witness to him, and above all the power of his redeeming work, which gives us a share in his Spirit. Earlier in this chapter (p 55f) we thought about the ways of describing the bond which unites those who have received Christ's offer of redemption; and we realised that one way to describe it is to say that it is like a family – a group of people joined by a common source of life. In this sense all christians are indeed a family; we are brothers, even if separated brethren.

The relationship between the various christian churches is so various and so complex that this is not the place to go into it. Briefly, all we need say here is this: that as catholics we do most unhesitatingly affirm that there is 'one Lord, one faith, one baptism', and that this gives us something in common with our fellow-christians which is more important than what divides us; that over and above this common basis in life, there are genuine aspects of the christian tradition

61

which have been conserved and fostered in different denominations, and that these denominations often bear witness to these facets of the full christian truth more clearly than the catholic church; but that the catholic church too bears witness to certain aspects of the truth, and that nothing essential to the church which Christ wants is utterly lacking in the catholic church.

We know that God is not absent from the world – that wherever there are men of good faith and good will, he is there even though unseen and unrecognised; but the christian recognises in the christian ideal the best example of the world God wants. And in the same way, we recognise in all christian communities the presence of Christ; but a catholic would hold that the catholic church, with all its imperfections, is at the moment the church nearest the church Christ wants. At the moment: because we hope and pray that the movement of the Spirit which is visible in the world today will lead to a church even closer to the mind and heart of Christ, and this will be a church unmarred by the present divisions.

The structure of the church

The church is the body of Christ; and the three implications of this which we have already discussed give us the key to the essential elements in its organisation. The fundamental structure of course is very simple: there is Christ who is the head, and all others who are his members. But the body is also a visible organisation and must visibly proclaim its structure as the body of Christ; that is to say, Christ's headship must be visibly proclaimed within the society. This is done in various ways in different situations, but it is particularly true in three essential aspects of the church's function – the three traditionally summed up under the headings of priest, prophet and king.

The church exists to carry on the work of Christ; and the climax of that work was the moment of redemption; and the day before he suffered, at a meal, he took bread and wine and said, 'This is my body, this is my blood shed for you; do this in memory of me'. The eucharist is full of meaning and a special chapter will be devoted to it later; but looked at from any point of view it is clear that in the eucharist the church is supremely engaged in its most essential role, reenacting as Christ's body the supreme act of Christ himself. He offered himself in love to the Father, and here we as members of his body offer ourselves in love. But if the church is acting as the body of Christ then the role of Christ the head must be visibly represented here; and that is the function of the ordained 'priest'. All of us who are baptised into Christ share his priest-hood. But the effectiveness of our priesthood flows from his; we offer ourselves because Christ made it possible for us to do so, our offering is pleasing to God because it is one with that of his own beloved Son. So here, where the body of Christ is acting 'in memory' of him, one of the priestly community steps forward as the visible representative of Christ renewing his own offering of himself, so that the offering of the whole body, head and members, may ascend as one in the sight of God.

Christ enters our world, the word of God, a sharp, two-edged sword (Heb 4:12), disruptive ('I have come to bring not peace but the sword') not in order to destroy but to challenge, to stir up the world from its lethargy of mediocrity and offer it the awful challenge of godhead. Christ is a prophet (see p 24f). He bears witness to the truth, not as an abstract body of information but as a reality, a life, a relationship with God. He then left his church, his body living with his life, to play the same part – to bear witness to the truth of

God in an alien world.

Of course the truth in this sense does involve truths in a more intellectual sense, truths we know. But these truths are still not an abstract body of information; they are the articulation of the reality which we live. It's rather like the difference between a set of mathematical problems and a biology text book. In the first case we can start with a purely theoretical abstract proposition and work out a series of deductions ('If x = 2, then 2x = 4'; and it doesn't matter what reality 'x' stands for, if any). Whereas a biology text book is an attempt to describe and explain the facts of life. The truths which the church has to proclaim are rather like this. The church lives with the life of God, and such teaching as it gives is an attempt to find words and concepts to express this life.

Moreover, Christ launched his church into the world, into history; it is itself involved in history, in time, in the ongoing world; it is not floating in some upper atmosphere serenely untouched by the events of history. The reality of the divine life to which the church bears witness is a reality which is lived in a human situation with all its vicissitudes. And it is in this situation that the church is engaged in the process of trying to understand itself. It is therefore subject to the same hesitations and difficulties as any other human institution, or any other human person. Doubt and dispute in the church are not exceptions, they are normal. The gift of infallibility does not mean that the church will never make any mistake; it means just what it says – it means that the church will never fail; it means that, unique amongst human institutions, it will never utterly cease to exist, never be totally untrue to its function. We have become familiar with the English translation of a phrase in the gospels: 'the gates of hell will not prevail against it'; but in the Greek it is the gates of *hades*, of *sheol*, the place of death; in other words, it does not mean that the church is impregnable to any assault of the devil, but that it is not subject to death and dissolution. It does not have a complete set of answers to human problems, a fully programmed series of responses.

It is true that the church does indeed arrive, sometimes after much agony and anxiety, at a clear understanding of certain aspects of her truth, and can define these as 'dogmas'. But dogmas are not a system of 'correct-think' or 'right-talk'. They may be regarded as mile-stones and sign-posts in the church's journey towards full truth. Mile-stones, because they do mark a definite acquisition, a definite stage in the journey. But sign-posts, because they point us onwards, they are never the last stage. Of the nature of the case, arrived at through long groping and after much consideration, they are always liable to be the answer to yesterday's problems rather than to today's and still less to tomorrow's. But they do mark the direction of our search and provide part of the data for our answer. In spite of all that we have said about the difficulties and ambiguities of the church's situation in the world, we are not 'tossed this way and that, and carried away with every wind of doctrine' (Eph 4:14). Standing firm on our past, we go forward into the future with these mile-stones and sign-posts to guide us.

This is the function of the church, continuing the prophetic role of Christ, bearing witness to the truth of the divine life in the world. We who are baptised into Christ, we who share his Spirit, we are prophets. But this function is not the prerogative of individual christians, nor of the collection of individual christians; it is the function of the body of Christ working through and with Christ the head of the body. And in its role as a visible body, Christ's headship is visibly represented in the body. This was done in the first place by the apostles, those who were with him 'from the preaching of John until the day he was taken from us, witnesses of the resurrection' (Ac 1:22, cf 10:41). They embodied their witness in the writings which now form the new testament; and the church will never stray from this basic witness to the historical Christ. But this was a beginning, not the end of the church's prophetic function. And the apostolic office of representing Christ, the chief prophet, has been handed on to those whom we call bishops[1]. This does not mean that they are the sole proclaimers of truth; but in the prophetic function which is the role of the whole body of Christ, they link the members to the head in virtue of a commission handed down ultimately from the visible head himself.

One aspect of the work of Christ which we call 'redemption' was unity – to bring people together to live in friendship and harmony with each other. For this purpose he formed a society which was to be the first sample of a world – a world in which discord, hatred and antagonisms would be replaced by harmony, love and unity. As we have already seen, this does not mean a dead conformity but the harmony of a rich, fruitful diversity. But in order to maintain this unity and diversity some unifying principle is needed. In society this role is played by government. In a civilised mature society government does not mean domination on the one hand and servile obedience on the other; the whim of authority and unquestioning conformity of the subjects. The point of government is its regulating and co-ordinating function, fostering the greatest possible freedom and opportunity for development for the members of the society.

This was certainly the role of the king in the old testament (cf p 28f) – to bring unity to the scattered tribes and disparate races. But this situation, which we have already considered, brings to light another point which bears on our present subject. The unity brought about by the monarchy was not a political arrangement, a treaty imposed by the victor on subject peoples or accepted by all parties for their mutual benefit. It was an acknowledgement and acceptance of a relationship with God which bound them together. It was a covenant, not a treaty. And the anointed king was the symbol and the focal point of this double unity – binding men to God and joining men to each other.

And this was the role of Christ, which we refer to when we speak of him as king. It is very easy to think first of all of domination and power in relationship to Christ's kingship; he is after all Lord of all, 'All power is given to me in heaven and on earth'. But it is precisely because his power is beyond challenge that it is beneath his dignity to assert it. He himself expressed most vividly his own view of authority: 'Among the pagans it is the kings who lord it over them, and those who have authority are given the title of benefactor. This must not happen to you. No; the greatest among you must behave as the one who serves. . . . You call me Lord and master, and rightly; for so I am. If I then have washed your feet, you should wash each other's feet' (Lk 20:24–30, Jn 13:13–14). His kingship is in the service of unity; but it is a unity based not on tyranny or even a benevolent despotism, but a unity of loving union with him: 'a unity in the work of service, building up the body of Christ, until we become the perfect man, fully mature with the fulness of Christ himself' (Eph 4:13). Unity with him, and through him, unity with God: 'He must be king until he has put everything under his feet; and the last enemy is death. Then will come the end when, having done away with all sovereignty, authority and power, he hands over the kingdom to God the Father, so that God may be all in all' (1 Cor 15:24–28).

This is the role of Christ the king; and this is the role of his body, the church – to be a magnet, a beacon, a sign of unity to the world. But in the body of Christ, Christ's own kingly role – the service of unity – is visibly represented. Just as amongst the apostles, Peter was selected to be the focal point of the unity of them all, so amongst the bishops the successor of Peter bears the burden of being the source and centre of the church's unity.

As we shall see later, the eucharist is the focal point of the church; the body of Christ which is the church is formed by the body of Christ in the sacrament; the church is a eucharistic community. But there are not many churches; there is only one body of Christ. The 'link man' between the various local churches which exist wherever mass is said is the bishop. One of the Latin words for a bishop is *pontifex*, which literally means 'bridge builder'; and the bishop is the one who joins together and unites the various churches in his diocese. The pope's title is *pontifex maximus*; he does on behalf of the whole church what the bishop does for the diocese – he is the bond and focal point of unity which joins them all into the one body of Christ.

Note:
(1) This is obviously not meant to be a complete treatment of the complex subject of scripture and tradition; it is merely meant to be an attempt to explain, to give a view of the place of bishops in the Church. For a fuller view one might see H. Kung, *Structures of the Church*, 1965, pp 158-200; Y. Congar, *Tradition and Traditions*, 1966, pp 328-338.

7

Prayer

Prayer is often regarded as something rather different from doctrine – as if doctrine were the public, official teaching of the faith, and prayer had to do with the private, devotional practice of it. Books which deal with doctrine sometimes omit it altogether, or put it in as a sort of appendix, as something extra. But if religion is the relationship between God and man, then prayer is clearly essential to it – is in fact merely another way of looking at the relationship, another form that it takes.

On the other hand, this is not the place to attempt any sort of spiritual direction on how to pray. What we want to do here is to give an account of what prayer is – what sort of an operation or activity or concept it is.

Probably the commonest way of looking at prayer is as a 'conversation' with God. This brings out the point that prayer is a personal communication; that it is not a 'magical' operation, as if simply by uttering the words, perhaps by finding the right words, we can hope somehow to achieve a desired effect; to describe it as a conversation brings out the fact that we communicate in a personal way with another person.

But this way of looking at it has its disadvantages too. In the first place, it is a rather curious sort of conversation where we cannot see the person we are talking to, where it is not quite clear to whom – or where – our words are addressed. It is like being shut in a completely dark room where you are assured someone is there but you have no idea where he is, in this corner or that or even behind your back. Similarly, it is a curious sort of conversation in which all the talking seems to be on one side. There is of course an easy answer to that difficulty, but it still remains true that the reply takes a different form from our part of the conversation. Then again there is the common idea that prayer means asking for things; probably the first meaning given to the word 'to pray' in any dictionary will be 'to beg, to beseech'. If we try to connect this with the idea of conversation, then this too gives a curious impression – a conversation which consists mainly of asking for things.

Of course it is quite easy to find an answer to all these difficulties. But the real difficulty lies much deeper. It lies in our attitude to our relationship with God. Religion is a personal relationship with God; but it is a relationship in which God first communicates with us, and we respond. Prayer is our response to God.

Our response

Prayer is our response to God. This is a very simple point, but it is often simply overlooked, and this is the source of much consequent confusion. It is our response; it is not an activity which we undertake in the first place, in which we take the initiative. God takes the initiative. When our Lord speaks to the woman of Samaria, she makes the prayer, 'Lord, give me to drink'; but it is he who begins the conversation, her prayer is merely the echo of his opening request, 'Woman, give me to drink' (Jn 4:7-15). 'We do not know what to pray for nor how to pray; but the Spirit himself prays for us' (Rom 8:26). Prayer sometimes feels like shouting into a dark and empty void, badgering an unheeding God; we do not quite know where he is, but we utter our words, hoping somehow to catch his attention.

But God is never heedless. God is always there, always with us, always attentive to us, always giving, always speaking to us. Our first task is to hear, to learn to listen, and then to reply. Prayer, no matter how much it may seem to be our doing, is in fact always a response.

God speaks to us. We have already given some thought to this idea of God 'speaking', and have realised that it is a figure of speech; that what we are referring to is the fact that a personal God enters into personal communication with us. We mean that God expresses himself (that he is not inert, passive, withdrawn in himself), and in his self-expression he communicates with us. So wherever God expresses himself he is communicating with us − everywhere, in everything that he does, in the whole of creation.

When the word 'creation' is used, we are inclined to think first of all of natural creation − earth, rivers, mountains, trees, stars; and secondly of God's initial act of creation, of bringing things out of non-being into being. But of course creation is not just something that God did, it is something that he does, something that is still going on today. And when man appears on the scene, he too has a part in this process. So that when we speak of creation we mean not merely the earth and sea and sky, but also houses, and streets, and motorways, and electricity pylons, and nuclear weapons. These are all part of creation, and it is here, in our highly complex world, that God is speaking to us.

Man's part in all of this is what may be called 'history'. In this too God speaks to us, in the events of human life. (One particular portion of history is of particular importance to us; it is the history of Israel, which is dealt with in the appendix, pp 108-111).

Creation means not only what God did in the beginning, but what God is doing now, including man's intervention in the process. This makes us realise that when we say that God 'speaks' to us in creation, it does not mean that he is simply giving us some information. When we say, for example, that 'the heavens declare the glory of God', we do not just mean that the heavens tell us about God's existence, his goodness, his power and his beauty. Communication means entering into communication with, entering into a personal relationship. So when we say that God communicates with us through the things he does, we mean that creation – our world, our environment, our circumstances, our situation – is the situation in which we are called to a personal relationship with God. It is a situation in which we are called to respond to God. God's communication with us is not a continual stream of information (and information given in a very obscure way, so that we are called on to crack the code before we can get the message). It is not a monologue, it is the first part of a dialogue.

God speaks, and we respond. And our response, in word or thought or deed, is 'prayer'. We respond to God as we hear his word – in our present situation, now. Prayer is always immediate, urgent. 'We hear his voice *today*' (Ps 95:7).

In the Spirit

All this urgent, immediate, ceaseless dialogue with God takes place within us. When we pray we are not hurling words into the void; we are speaking to God who is with us. And when we say 'within us' this does not mean that prayer takes place in the loneliness of my empty skull. We mean in the depths of my being, 'deeper than heart or head'; in my very spirit, where the Spirit of God dwells. By the very fact that God made us in his image, and even more by the fact that he has recreated us by redemption, this almighty, infinite God has made his home in us. This is what our Lord tells us, in the name of the whole Trinity: 'We will come and take up our abode with him' (Jn 14:23). We say that God invites us to a personal relationship with him. But we have seen that God is three-personal, so that we are called to a threefold relationship with him; to the Father who is the source of our being, to the Son who shares our being, to the Spirit through whom we share the being of God. Our personal relationship with God is rooted in the depths of our personality. It is through our situation, through the world around us that God speaks to us; but the dialogue actually begins and ends in our being.

Prayer, therefore (especially mental prayer, meditation, contemplation), can often seem like introspection or rumination, day-dreaming. And indeed it very well might be; it is a danger we have to be aware of. But the reverse may be equally true; for a christian, living in the presence and power of God, the simple process of thinking may be a form of prayer. And certainly true prayer will eventually spring from and centre on the intimate core of one's personality. This is what St Paul says in the passage quoted above: 'We do not know what to pray for, nor how to pray for it; but the Spirit himself prays for us with wordless pleading' (Rom 8:26). This does not mean confining or limiting God, bringing him down to our level. He is still 'other', beyond what our minds can conceive. Only he is not remote and distant or beyond our reach.

And it is from our spirit that we respond to God. Just as the whole person of God enters into a personal relationship with us, so we respond with our whole personality.

We bring to our dialogue with God our appreciation

and awareness of all that God has done; and we respond with adoration and thanksgiving (cf pp 102f). But creation is not yet complete, and our response is not simply a passive contemplation of its beauty. We are called to echo God's creative word, we are called to share the work of creation; and our creativity is part of our response to God. We are called, too, to share God's redeeming word in Christ ('I have come that they may have life, and have it more abundantly'); we are called not only to make a contribution to the progress of the world, but to make the world into the kingdom of God. This then involves the prosaic work of planning, of thinking what to do; and this in turn brings awareness of our incapacity and our need; this too is our response to God, this is prayer.

But our response is not only joy and thanksgiving, and eager desire to continue God's work. The world speaks to us – or God through the world speaks to us – not only of beauty and life, but also of ugliness and evil; and our response takes the form of sorrow, and bitter acknowledgement of failure, and a yet more urgent realisation of our need. But we also accept the suffering which is part of the world not yet fully redeemed, and in union with the redemptive suffering of Christ this too becomes fruitful, and part of our response to God.

Prayer and prayers

Wherever our response to God is, there is prayer. It is not a separate, special part of our lives, even of our religious lives. The activity often called 'saying our prayers' would perhaps be better thought of as means to prayer – ways of concentrating and focussing and stimulating our response.

But we do need such aids. The Holy Spirit is with our spirit, but when we look into ourselves we do not find the Spirit enthroned there in undisputed sway; our minds and hearts are flooded with confused and conflicting desires clamouring for priority. Christian tradition has developed a number of 'techniques' for focussing our response to God; and in recent years other 'techniques' from eastern cultures (Zen, or Yoga, for example) have also attracted interest. These may be none the less helpful because they come from a different tradition. They remind us of factors in our response to God which have been overlooked in the western tradition, or which have become stereotyped and lifeless. 'Close your eyes and join your hands', for example, has become such a cliché that it would often be greeted with derision nowadays – even though it is in fact only a way of stressing the need to withdraw from 'outward' distractions to concentrate on one's 'inner self', and that our bodily posture can be an aid to directing our mental state.

Probably the commonest of the 'Aids to prayer' is still the use of prayer-formulae, certain forms of words which have been found to be useful in summing up our unformed desires and in guiding and inspiring our own thoughts. The bible, the word of God in a special sense; especially the life of Christ, the Word made flesh; hymns, and even secular literature; as well as such formulae as the rosary, the 'Our Father', and all the 'prayers' which we found in all the many books of prayers: these are all ways in which we may find it easier to hear God's word to us and through which our own response to that word may be stimulated.

It goes without saying that the point of all these 'aids' is not the mere recitation of the words, and that they are pointless if they do not in some way express our personal response. But there is a particular difficulty about public prayers. Children are often confused and scandalised by having to recite prayers far too quickly for their minds to assimilate the words –

until they sadly come to accept it as one of the many contradictions in religion. But public prayer is a part of our lives. When we say that prayer is a personal response, when we say that it is a part of our personal relationship with God, we do not mean that it must exclude other people. On the contrary, we mean that it is the response of our whole persons; and our persons are linked with others (cf p 14). If we bring our whole being to God in prayer, it means that we come to him in the whole complex web of relationships in which our being is involved.

Public prayer, then, is an essential part of our response to God in prayer. But any corporate act imposes its own limitations. A group of people together cannot act exactly as if each one was on his own; if one person is occupying a certain chair, another person has to take another. So in public prayer, for example, we have to use an agreed form of words; and inevitably this form will not be the way each person would put it individually. Sometimes (as at mass) one individual will voice the prayer on behalf of the whole community; and again, his way of uttering it will not suit everyone. And if the whole community recite a prayer together, each individual will have to moderate his speed, his volume, his expressiveness to take account of the group. Public prayer is in fact a rather different sort of activity from private prayer. It is essentially a corporate act. We are expressing much more our presence as a group than our private dialogue with God.

And yet of course the form in which we express our sense of community does mean something – we do not come together to pray and then recite 'The Wreck of the Hesperus', we cannot say that it doesn't matter what we do as long as we do it together. So there is undoubtedly something of a dilemma here: corporate prayer means subjecting one's private needs and desires to those of the group; and yet if it is to be genuine prayer, it must express our personal response to God. But at least this is true – that if we have never thought about the words, if we have never at any time tried to make them our own, or if the very act of public recitation does not lead us to take them to ourselves, then it is difficult to see the value of it (and it would be true to say that we might as well recite 'The Wreck of the Hesperus'). Public prayer, in other words, always has a reference to private prayer; the former takes its value from the latter, it is a brief flash of light from the light we have found in these words, in our moments of silent communion with the Spirit.

The prayer of Christ

Our Lord himself is obviously our model for prayer, as he is of our whole christian life: and there is one passage in the gospels which gives us a particularly deep insight into the most intimate relationship of Christ with his Father. It is that occasion when he has cured a paralysed man (Jn 5:1-15), and he explains that this is not really so very extraordinary, that it is the sort of thing to be expected of him since he is the Son of the life-giving Father; and he goes on:

> The Son cannot do anything
> But what he sees the Father doing;
> For the Father loves the Son
> And shows him whatever he does.

Sees . . . shows; in these few words we are given a glimpse of what we might call the interior life of our Lord. The Father is the source of life, of all that is; but in creating he 'shows' the Son what he is doing – lays bare his mind and heart and will. And for the Son similarly, the world is not simply an accumulation of facts and phenomena; they speak to him of his Father, he 'sees' what the Father does. Father and Son are rapt in contemplation of each other. For Jesus, it is not simply a matter of a casual glance towards God in the midst of a busy life; his mental gaze is fixed unswervingly on his Father seen in all he does.

It is from this contemplation that the action of Jesus springs – actions like the curing of the paralytic. His actions are not the servile obedience of a slave; nor are they a mechanical copying of this perfect model. 'The Father *loves* the Son, and so shows him. . .' Their mutual contemplation is a gaze of love, and this loving contemplation informs the very being of the Son, so that his action is that 'natural' continuation of the Father's: 'My Father works until now, and I work' (5:17). And it is a continuation, not simply a repetition; our Lord does not leave his Father's work as he found it – he cures the cripple. But his work is the continuation of the life-giving power of his Father's creative act. Each mind, the Father's and the Son's, responds perfectly to the other; each will is in perfect unison; and so the action of the Son fulfills his Father's will.

This is the ideal which we are striving to attain, unsuccessfully, in our christian life, and particularly in our prayer. We are not trying, independently of God, to make our actions conform to his law; nor are we trying in prayer to bring him to change his mind, to change his world, to perform miracles for us. We are trying to see into the mind and heart of God, so that our actions *will* be like his. We are not trying to bend his will to ours, but to learn what he is like, raising our minds to his. We are trying 'to see him more clearly, to love him more dearly, to follow him more nearly'.

8

Sacraments

'No man has ever seen God: the only-begotten
has revealed him to us' (Jn 1:18)

It is by no means unique to the christian religion to
visualise two levels of reality – an upper and a lower,
the visible and the invisible, the divine and the human.
But the doctrine of the incarnation means that in the
person of Jesus this distinction has been obliterated. In
him 'the fullness of the godhead dwelt in human form'
(Col 2:9); and in him, then, God dealt with men at the
human level; he acted in a human way, acted and
reacted, entered into communication with men as men
do with each other. There was no pretence or play-
acting in the human existence of Jesus, and in him
God was involved in the very fibre of human existence.
To achieve communication with other men he did not
work some superhuman kind of thought-transference;
to achieve what he wanted he did not simply silently
and powerfully will it; he spoke, he smiled, he
stretched out his hand. And finally he suffered, he
sweated, he bled, he died; and in that body he came
back to life. It was by the reality of his human existence that human existence has been changed.

This is the very basis of what we mean by a sacrament. 'A sacrament is an outward sign of inward
grace'; but what we mean is that God acts with men,
among men, in a human way; not out of condescension

for our human weakness, not as a method of teaching, a sort of clever visual aid; but because these are the terms of human existence. 'God so loved the world . . .'; but that love was expressed in a visible, tangible way, just as we express our love for others; just as a mother, for example, not only feels love towards her child, not only 'thinks' love towards her child, but actually feeds it. This is what we mean by a sacrament; and in this sense, Christ himself in his human existence is the sacrament of God. The invisible God has appeared amongst us in human form, in Jesus; he has expressed his love for us in the human words and deeds of Jesus.

Christ then left the visible company of human life. But as we have seen he left behind him a 'body'; a group of human beings possessing his life, organically linked with him, and able to act visibly and effectively in a human environment as he himself had done. Christ is the sacrament of God, the visible and effective sign of God's love; and the church is the sacrament of Christ.

When we speak of the sacraments, then, it is of the church itself that we think in the first place. Otherwise – if we begin with the seven traditional sacraments and consider them on their own – it is very difficult to avoid the almost magical attitude that distorts so much of our thinking on this subject. The church is the sacrament of Christ, prolonging and continuing Christ's own function of bringing God into contact with men in their visible earthly reality. Therefore in a way all the activities of the church are 'sacramental' – all the good works that are carried out by the church, the proclamation of truth, the struggle for freedom, the concern for suffering. But two other points have to be taken into account. First of all, it must be clear that it is the church we are talking about – not the individual members of the church. We can really speak of sacraments only when the church is acting officially in its capacity as the body of Christ, when Christ the head of the body is visibly represented, acting on his authority (this is what we mean when we say that the sacraments are 'instituted by Christ'). Individual members of the church may be uniquely involved – as in marriage for example – but what makes it a sacrament is that they are involved here as representatives of the church.

Secondly, the sacraments are not exclusive but, so to speak, typical. In any life – in our Lord's life – although all the actions are really those of the person acting, nevertheless some actions are more 'typical' than others, more expressive of the essential nature of the person. We are familiar with this in our own experience – when we say of somebody, 'That's typical; that's just like them'. When our Lord made a casual friendly remark to the people he was with, or when he took off his sandals, these were undoubtedly the actions of the Son of God; but equally undoubtedly they are not so meaningful, so 'revealing', so expressive of his real personality as his passion, death and resurrection. And in the same way, although all the actions of the church are sacramental because they flow from her sacramental nature, we do recognise that we can use the word 'sacrament' especially of certain specific activities in which this nature is more specifically involved.

Of course other actions of the church or the activity of individual members of the church may be just as valuable as sacramental acts; but their value is always connected with the sacramental acts. For example the life-long love and loyalty of married people is much more important than the marriage ceremony; but it is the sacrament of marriage which flows into and finds expression in the daily devotion of the married couple. A sacrament is a sign; and one characteristic of a sign is that although it may be a single object or action, it is a summary and a concentration of a much wider field of experience. Isn't this the whole point of art – that the poet or the painter uses images which mean much more than they say; which sum up and crystallise a world of meaning, which are 'evocative'. And in the same way, the sacrament of penance for example is not the only means of forgiveness or the only moment of repentance for christians; but it sums up all our desire for forgiveness and in one dramatic act sets in operation God's willingness to forgive.

Or to put it another way, the sacraments are the language of the christian community. A community is formed by communication. This is the function of language – not only to express our ideas, but to enable us to express them in a form which can be transmitted to others, to enable us to share the common pool of experience of the community of which we are part. There is no reason why we should call a tree 'a tree' except that this is the way that members of a particular group of people have agreed to designate this object. A rose by any other name would smell as sweet; it wouldn't make any difference to the flower itself if you decided to call it 'a washing machine'; the only thing is that it would lead to difficulty in communication with other people. In fact people sometimes do invent their own language; fond couples might have their own private endearments, or a secret society might have its codes and passwords. But this language still serves as a means of communication, to be used by members of this particular community.

But words are not the only form of language; we can communicate by signs as well. Sometimes the signs are an imperfect substitute for words, as you realise when you're trying to ask the way in a foreign country; but sometimes they are a much more effective way of communicating – think of a mother feeding her child, or a handshake between friends, or a kiss. And one way of thinking about the sacraments is as the language of the christian community, the sign-language by which the community is formed, the means we use to express and deepen our membership of this community.

The catholic church holds that there are seven sacraments – seven aspects of the church's activity as officially re-enacting Christ's great redemptive act. Their significance is fairly clear and most catholics do in fact understand them well enough. Here I would like to consider briefly some aspects on which there may appear to have been a change of stress.

Sacraments of initiation

There are three sacraments which affect the very basis of the christian life, the making of a christian. These are baptism, confirmation and the eucharist.

When we say that Christ made the divine life available to men, it would be more accurate to say that he made it available to specific men. We are after all dealing with a historical situation; our Lord lived, died and rose again at a specific moment in time and at a certain place. And it was to a specific group of people that his gift of new life was made available, those who had been with him during his life. They were given the new life by his direct gift, 'baptised in the Holy Spirit'. This group was then formed into the body of Christ; and after his ascension they were empowered to act with his authority and to offer others the same life. They did this by the ritual act of baptism (why, we shall see in a moment). The others so embraced by this life were then in turn incorporated into his body and enabled to offer it to yet others, and so on down to ourselves and the youngest child baptised today.

So it is the church which brings this life to us; not Christ directly but the church acting visibly, tangibly in his name and with his authority, in virtue of its union with Christ the head of the body. The church is like a mother, bringing forth children in Christ. Or to look at it another way (which our earlier discussion of the church may make clearer), the church is a nation, a society, a new race of mankind, in which the atmosphere men breathe is the atmosphere of redemption; into this new society, this new 'social environment', baptism initiates us. (This too may give us some insight into the practice of infant baptism. The child cannot itself take part in the 'sign-language' of the christian community, any more than at a human level a child can seek or reject the chance to be born; but the child is lovingly offered the gift of life, and is guaranteed the care which will enable it to live and grow in society. Of course as the child grows it will have to develop the life it has and assert its membership of the community. The child may in fact reject it, as growing children do reject the society in which they were brought up. But in the meanwhile this child has the right of a chance to live, and the community undertakes to provide the means by which it can grow to maturity in Christ).

The apostles received the new life, the Spirit of God, directly; after all, they had experienced direct contact with Christ in his human life. But when they came to hand it on, they did so by appropriate sign-language. What they were 'saying' was this: by Christ's death and resurrection, you are now able to die to your previous life and to live with the life of God; here is death and life made available to you. To communicate this, they used the symbol of water. It is a symbol which is rich in meaning at a purely natural, human level: the tumultuous, overwhelming ocean and the surging waters of the flood are a symbol of danger and death, and at the same time water is one of the basic requirements for life[1]. But it is also a symbol which was particularly meaningful in the story of God's dealings with men – it would recall above all the waters of the Red Sea through which God first led his people from the slavery of Egypt to the new life of freedom as sons of God. It was with this in mind that our Lord refers to his own death as a 'baptism': 'I have a baptism to be baptised with, and how am I constrained until it is accomplished' (Lk 12:50); his death was like being submerged in 'a sea of sorrows'. But his death was a source of life; and this too was expressed in the same symbol of water – 'a spring of water welling up to eternal life' (Jn 4:14). Death and life: by this symbol the power of Christ's death and resurrection are applied to the new christian.

But as we have already seen, redemption is such a rich reality that it is impossible really to tie it down to one single moment or action of our Lord's life. His death and resurrection certainly are the key factor in redemption; but at the moment of his birth the human situation was transformed by the very fact that God had become man; and at the ascension, too, this humanity was enthroned with God. But the sending of the Spirit, too, which the scriptures associate with the feast of Pentecost, is an essential element in the complete work of redemption. 'God raised Jesus to life, and now, raised to the heights by God's right hand, he has received the Holy Spirit; and what you see and hear is the outpouring of that Spirit' (Ac 2:33). Christ has conquered death, and the dynamic power of divine life has full, untramelled play in him – that life which was symbolised by the wind in the old testament. He has this life, and he gives it to us.

But what Christ did, the church does. The church is not only the receiver of the Spirit, but the giver; it is a redeemed but also a redeeming community. It is not only filled with the Spirit for its own private benefit, but – like Christ; because it is the body of Christ – it possesses this Spirit in order to spread it throughout the world. And to be a full member of the body of Christ is not merely to live with his Spirit but to share his life-giving role, his role as sender of the Spirit. Confirmation is the sacrament by which the community of Christ formally and officially initiates the christian into this role as sender of the Spirit, as one responsible for playing a part in the church's redeeming activity.

This sacrament is sometimes spoken of as the sacrament of christian maturity, the sacrament of catholic action, a sacrament which makes us 'soldiers of Christ'. These ideas certainly have some value; but they may be misleading unless they are taken with the more basic idea – the role of the church which like Christ – with Christ – sends forth the Spirit, and the role of the individual christian as a member of this church.

The christian community lives through the Spirit of God, which is a Spirit of love; and in that self-giving love it exists to be (we are still dealing with the very basis of the christian life) a sign and a sacrament of unity – unity with all men, with each other, with Christ, with God. The eucharist is the sacrament which expresses this aspect of the church's existence. But this sacrament is important enough to call for separate treatment in the next chapter.

Sacraments of the community

Since all the sacraments are actions of the community, it may seem out of place to describe two in particular – marriage and orders – as community sacraments. But it is true that in these two the social aspect is more evident. Or one might put it this way, that in the other sacraments the community acts in relationship to individual christians, whereas individuals are called on in these to represent the community.

It is precisely not our purpose here to say everything that could be said about every doctrine; on the contrary, we want to restrict ourselves to those topics on which there may be some doubt or hesitation about where new trends in christian thinking fit in with the established pattern of doctrine. So these two sacraments can be passed over here. The sacrament of orders has already been touched on in dealing with the church; and the sacrament of marriage is well catered for in many good books.

The sacraments of the fall

This too may be thought a curious way of referring to sacraments. This way of describing them is merely used to draw attention to a strange, disconcerting feature of our christian life. The church is spoken of in such glowing terms in christian tradition – the bride of Christ, holy, unspotted, without flaw or blemish; a loving mother, wise, merciful, seeking with tender concern those she has begotten; and we sometimes think she must live in Rome, or else in heaven – because none of this seems to apply to the church we are familiar with, and certainly not to ourselves. Or again we speak of the work of Christ and all he has done for us – he has overcome death and put an end to the state in which men lived – a state of slavery, ignorance, sin and death, and set us free to live as sons of God. We say all this; and then we look around us at the sad reality and wonder what these phrases mean.

We have already dealt with this to some extent when we were discussing 'sin' and 'the church' (and both of those sections should be in our mind in the present subject). Certainly, all that we have been saying is true of our Lord himself, and we would not find it too difficult to apply also to those heroic souls who have followed his call with absolute fidelity. But if we ask why it is not true of everyone, we would have to think yet again about what our Lord came to do. He came to save us, we say; but we realise that this is a short-hand formula. A more careful statement would be that he came to make it possible for us to make the world into a place fit for sons of God. This differs from the short formula on three points. First, our Lord's work is not simply concerned with men, but with the whole world, the whole of creation. Secondly, however, mankind does have an essential role in this work; we are made in the image of God, we are able to respond freely to God's action, to co-operate with him in remaking the world; and an essential aspect of Christ's work was the redemption of mankind as a stage in his redemption of the world. But thirdly, we don't say he redeemed man, but that he made redemption a possibility. He didn't simply redeem man – put him in a redeemed state, transform him whether he wanted it or not. He didn't do this; he couldn't. Man was made by God with the capacity for free choice, and this is essential to man, it is what makes a man a man; so that if our Lord had simply transformed man into another type of being, even though it might be a higher type of being, he would have been destroying what he made. Almighty God, we might say, was faced with a choice – to have men who were free and therefore free to go against his wishes, or men who conformed perfectly to his wishes but were not free. And of course he chose the first; he had to, because if they conformed without being free, they would not really have been human at all.

But once we see this, we are not surprised that the world – the redeemed world – is far from perfect. But this is not to say that Christ didn't do anything. He did make it possible for us to share the divine life, far above anything we could have achieved by ourselves. And when we say that he made it possible for us, we mean a real possibility, not just a theoretical possibility. Baptism, and its comparison with human birth, may make it easier for us to see this. If we ask whether a child is a perfect human being, the answer is of course not; the child can't walk properly, can't co-ordinate its movements, can't talk intelligibly; there are all sorts of potentialities in the child which have to be developed before it can be said to be a satisfactory specimen of what a human being can be. But the potentialities are there. The child is not like a baby chimpanzee which no matter how carefully nurtured and educated will never grow up to be a Beethoven or a Picasso or a Shakespeare. In the same way, Christ's action has planted in us the seed of divine life with the capacity to grow into the full maturity of sons of God.

Christ did not magically produce in the whole human race a fully redeemed state; he gave us the power to become fully redeemed. And just as a child – most children – fail to develop their potentialities fully, so do most sons of God.

We fail. We fail both in our personal sins and in our task of working out Christ's redemption in the world. We fail where Christ succeeded; but he did succeed, and his work survives and continues, and our failures do not normally utterly undo the work of Christ either in ourselves or in the society which shares his life. It is this ambiguity, that we are imperfect members of the glorious body of Christ, that is the basis of what we have called 'the sacraments of the fall'. We fail and it is as members of the body of Christ that we fail. If the church is less than perfect, it is our failures which have contributed to making it so; if the church is not the splendid ideal of perfect humanity, it is partly our fault; we have blurred and obscured 'the sign'; we have blocked the channel of overflowing life and love that comes from God through Christ to the world. Therefore it is to the church that we come to confess our sinfulness and receive reconciliation. If it were merely a question of our individual relationship with God we need only ask him for forgiveness – hardly that even; for no matter how much we turn away from God, he does not turn away from us, and to be received back into his love we need only turn back to him to find him waiting there with open arms to receive us [2]. But we do not stand before God as individuals, but as members of his body. So it is to the church and in the church, above all to Christ as head of the church, that we confess.

We confess: we *profess* our sinfulness; we make a clear, honest, open avowal of our failure, not a grudging, mumbling, hesitant admission that we have been less than perfect. It is a healthy opportunity to be honest with oneself. Of course this does not mean that each confession will involve interminable, neurotic soul-searching about exact numbers of offences and the precise degree of guilt in each. It is not so much a question of individual sins for which we seek forgiveness; it is rather our sinfulness which we are recognising and regretting. We are not saying merely that we have sinned, but that we are sinners; and the individual sins which we mention are merely like the tip of an iceberg, samples of our failure through which we make concrete our awareness of our sinfulness. Sin is a breach of personal relationship with God, and how much of our personality is involved in individual acts is difficult to decide.

We fail; we all fail; and if we are not already conscious of this, the sacrament brings us face to face with Christ, by whose standard our failure becomes obvious. Christ is represented by his minister. One sometimes hears people say that this priest is very hard in confession (and therefore to be avoided if possible) while the other priest is very easy. But this seems to be a misunderstanding of the minister's role. It is no part of the priest's task either to condemn or to excuse a penitent. The priest in confession plays a prophetic role, proclaiming God's word not in praise or blame but so that the penitent may judge himself by that word. His task is to try to hold up the mirror of the divine image to us to help us to see ourselves in that light. By that light we all fail. But there is nothing in this either for complacency or for despair. The majesty of the vision of God does indeed make us aware of our poverty of spirit; but it is also a gaze of love and mercy. In this sacrament we encounter Christ who alone has the right to judge, but who promises love. Confession is above all an act of hope – of real, theological hope; time after time we come to this sacrament after repeated experience of failure, and where human reason would urge us to abandon the struggle, we here pledge ourselves to continue. It is indeed an encounter with Christ: we stretch out our hand in utter awareness of our need, and we touch Christ's hand outstretched to save.

But it is not only in our moral failures that the ambiguity of our redeemed status can be seen; it is seen too in the imperfection of the world in which we live, in poverty, suffering, sickness and death. These too were Christ's concern; in fact the gospels present him to us much more often healing the sick than forgiving sins. The church continues Christ's redeeming activity in our concern for all the world's needs: we are concerned, and as christians must be concerned, with education, medicine, housing, famine relief, the underdeveloped countries and so on. And this total concern with the redemption of the world is expressed sacramentally in the anointing of the sick. Here, in a symbolic way, Christ's will to heal is set in motion.

But Christ has also shown that suffering is not simply misfortune, something we must passively accept and tolerate as patiently as we can. In his hands, it became a triumphant assertion of the victory of love over hatred, of good over evil. And the sick, suffering, helpless and humiliated, cut off from any other form of activity, have imprinted on them through this sacrament the redeeming sufferings of Christ, and their suffering is taken up into the pattern of redemption.

The sacrament, then, is a reassurance to this sick person that Christ wills the healing of all our ills and that meanwhile our suffering is, like his, the means by which evil is conquered. But this sick person will die. The sacrament of anointing does contribute to the physical welfare of a sick person; but even if it does, even if it does so several times, the time will certainly come when it will not do so, and we shall die. But then the final meaning of the sacrament is brought into effect. For a christian, life is not taken away but changed. We do believe in eternal life, we do believe that we pass through death to life. And this anointing, like Mary's anointing of Christ, is 'anointing for burial', a pledge that we like Christ will rise again triumphant over death.

Note:
1 Although we are concerned only with doctrine here, nevertheless one might briefly note this illustration of what was said earlier (p 8) about 'integration'. The theme of 'water' is one which is familiar to any teacher – familiar, necessary and easy. In dealing with this rich theme, it seems artificial to exclude the religious significance of water from the teacher's mind or teaching; and on the other hand, the religious significance is there precisely because of its significance in life. One may note too how impoverished is the idea that baptism means 'washing'. To say that baptism 'washes away original sin' is certainly true – just as it is obviously true that water is used for washing; but it is equally obvious that this is not the only use for water, nor even its main value. If you say that baptism only washes, you are saying that sin is only a black mark, and to be a christian is just to be clean;

whereas to be a christian is so much more than this; it is a life, and sin is the absence of this life. You don't bring a dead baby to life by giving it a bath; and you don't make a child of God just by washing it.

2 This is all we need to do; but it is not as easy as it sounds. Sins blind and bind us so that the simple act of 'turning back' may become psychologically much more difficult. From this point of view too the practice of confession may be valuable. Its psychological value has often been pointed out – the value of externalising our failures, giving them explicit expression, not repressing them; and the reassurance of forgiveness expressly formulated by the minister. This is not being ignored here, but it is already well known and it is less important.

9

The eucharist

'Let us proclaim the mystery of faith.'

The word 'mystery' is used here, not in the sense of 'mysterious' – so mysterious that it cannot be understood but only believed – but in the more traditional sense that we have touched on previously (cf p 12f). It is the word used when the invisible God comes into our world, so that visible and tangible realities become the means by which we come into contact with him. It is a synonym for another technical term, the term 'sacrament'[1]; visible realities – human words and actions and visible materials – become the sign by which an invisible effect takes place.

'Faith' too is a word which has a variety of meanings, some narrower, some wider. In the narrower sense it is often used to denote the act by which we hold certain propositions to be true on the authority of God revealing. But we also commonly use it in a wider sense as almost a synonym for 'religion'. We are really using it that way when we speak of 'the catholic faith': we do not mean merely the sum-total of the things which a catholic believes; we mean the whole system and pattern of life which we call catholic.

It is in this latter sense that the word is used here. The eucharist is 'the mystery of faith': it is the sacrament in which the whole of our religion is summed up; in this one rite the whole of our relationship with God

94

is contained.

It is not surprising, then, that the eucharist can so often appear to be a confusing topic. It has too much meaning to be assimilated all at once, and we tend to seize on some particular aspect and say, '*This* is the point'. The miracle of the real presence: that this is not just bread and wine, but our Lord's body, blood, soul and divinity – that's the point, someone will say. And someone else will say, no, not simply the miracle of transubstantiation, but the mass; the reenactment of our Lord's own sacrifice. And someone else will say, what about the resurrection? Isn't this too an essential part of Christ's redemptive act? and this too must be represented here.

One could go on almost indefinitely identifying and stressing different aspects – different aspects of the whole, almost boundless, truth. And we in our turn cannot really hope to do full justice to the full truth, especially if we wish to keep within the desired bounds of brevity. What we can do is to present a way of looking at it which, while remaining simple, will take into account as many aspects as possible.

Bread and wine

We start with what is most obvious about this sacrament – the bread and wine. After all, it *is* a sacrament, a physical reality through and in which divine reality is conveyed to us, and this physical, visible element is meant to convey the meaning to us. If someone completely strange to our ways and customs came into church during a wedding, he would have no difficulty in seeing that the ceremony was essentially concerned with a man and a woman. If a complete stranger were present at a baptism, he should have no difficulty in seeing that essentially what happens is that water is poured over a child, and you could explain to him what it is all about by explaining what water means to us. And if that same stranger were present during mass it should be quite clear that the essential elements in the ceremony are bread and wine which are consumed. It is, in other words, a meal.

Of course, it is a symbolic meal – it is not a real feast at which everyone simply tucks in to a well-laden table. But this is a quite normal feature in our society. When you 'drink a toast', you do not empty your glass; you just take a token sip. When a dignitary 'lays the foundation' of a building, he does not do a job of bricklaying; a symbolic gesture with a trowel is all that is expected. This 'symbolic gesture' is particularly appropriate in commemorative events. In a play, for example, attempts to stage a battle can become ridiculous if the producer actually tries to reenact a battle; in Shakespeare's *Henry V* we do not expect a blow-by-blow version of the battle of Agincourt; a token flurry of arms and confusion is enough to allow us to enter into the spirit of the occasion. Actually, it seems that the eucharist was sometimes taken in the context of a normal meal; St Paul describes the Lord's supper as a real meal, where people ate and drank, even to excess (1 Cor 11:20-22). But this is by no means necessary. To eat a morsel of bread, to take a sip of wine, this is all we need to make it a meal.

What we have to think of first, then, in thinking about the eucharist, is eating and drinking. But this is something which is of very deep significance in human life and society; so basic that it is almost banal to go into it in detail. Food is life; if we do not eat we die. Food is pleasure; a feast means joy and merry-making. Food is work; what we eat is the result of our labours. It is such a central part of life that in moments of cynicism we sometimes feel that we work to provide the food which gives us the strength to go on working . . . in a vicious circle. This is not true – life is much more than this – but it is true that food plays such an important part in life that it stands as a fitting symbol for the whole. Our joys and sorrows, labour and achievement – it is all summed up in food.

Because of this, eating food in common – a meal – has such significance. It is not merely an occasion when we jointly refuel our energies. To take food together implies a sharing of one's goods, sharing joys and sorrows, and even sharing life. To sit down at table together is automatically a sign of friendship and trust (to betray one with whom you take a meal is traditionally the blackest treachery). This is why any occasion for celebration – birthdays, weddings, any success or joy, and even an occasion of sorrow like a funeral – is marked by a meal. We may not often think of this when we invite someone to have a cup of coffee or when we are invited to dinner, but at a deeper level than habit or convention, this significance is present.

A community is formed by communication (cf p 82); and communication takes place not only by words but by signs, by actions, by gestures. Communication means not merely giving information; it means sharing of life, the means by which human community is established and expressed. Nowhere is this truer than in a meal; it is a sharing of life, a communication – a communion – which brings about community.

It is a secondary point but one which has its own importance, that a meal not only establishes a bond between those who eat together, but also points to our oneness with the world in which we live. The food we eat comes from that world, and as it becomes part of us so we become one with the earth from which it comes. In these days when so much of our food comes from tins, it is still true that ultimately it comes from the earth. The bread made from the wheat which grows from the soil, wine from the grapes ripened in the sun, water from the river, meat from the animals which graze in the field – this is what enters into us and nourishes our life.

The Lord's supper

In the eucharist, then, we are taking part in a meal – one of the commonest, simplest, and most profoundly significant of human occasions; and all that we have been saying applies also to *this* meal.

But this is a special meal. It is a meal taken 'in memory of Christ'. Many scholars today draw attention to the importance of meals in general in the early church's thinking about the eucharist. The fourth gospel describes an incident just after the resurrection (ch 21), when the apostles returned to their familiar role as fishermen; and after a fruitless night, a figure appeared on the shore and directed them to a catch which filled their nets. They then recognised the Lord, hurried ashore; and found a meal prepared for them. They ate – they ate in joy in the company of their risen Lord. When later they were celebrating the eucharist, would it not be of incidents like this that they would think? And again one of the gospels describes how two of the disciples after the death of Christ were going to a village called Emmaus, filled with sorrow at his recent death; they were joined by a mysterious stranger who roused them by explaining how this death fulfilled the scriptures; they invited him to stay for a meal with them; and they recognised him 'in the breaking of bread'. 'The breaking of bread': this is almost a technical term for the eucharist in Acts; but it is a useless subtlety discussing whether or not this meal at Emmaus was a 'eucharist' in the technical sense. It is surely sufficient to say that each time they celebrated the eucharist it was an occasion like this one – when after the sadness of separation came the joy of sharing; they ate a meal with him, with all that this implied, as they had so often done during his life.

Nevertheless, it is true that the eucharist refers specifically to one particular meal – the meal he took with his disciples the night before he died, ordering them to 'do this in memory of me'.

What then was *that* meal? What went on that night? The gospels merely say 'he gave thanks'; the whole account of the supper takes only a few lines in the first three gospels. But we realise that this is not meant to be by any means a full acount of every word our Lord said: and if we look at the fourth gospel – which, incidentally, does not give an account of the institution of the eucharist – we find that it devotes no less than five chapters to the conversation that night. Even this gospel, of course, does not attempt to give us a verbatim account, but using the gospels can we attempt to put ourselves into the situation?

If our Lord was a normal man – and he was – we would presume that part of the conversation at table that night was reminiscence: 'Do you remember the time that . . . and how . . .?' But we may presume also that this reminiscence was infused with a spirit of joy and gratitude to God. Moreover, on such a solemn occasion the conversation would surely not be confined to purely personal reminiscence, no matter how natural and affectionate, of all that they had experienced together ('you are the men who have stood by me faithfully in my trials', Lk 22:28); our Lord would see this in the context of all God's other blessings, in the world and in history, which they would remember with joy.

Remembering, joy, gratitude: this is practically a description of what the gospels call *eucharistia*, giving thanks. When they say that our Lord took bread and 'gave thanks' or 'blessed it', it does not mean simply a sort of grace before meals. It is a common – perhaps the commonest – form of prayer in the bible, sometimes called thanksgiving, sometimes praising, sometimes blessing; the *Magnificat* is another example of it. The basic idea underlying all these words (and we may add the word 'worship') could probably best be expressed by the word 'appreciation'. We are showing appreciation for God's goodness and greatness seen in the great things he has done. It is not simply that we are saying 'thank you' to God for what he has given us (we remember the cynic's definition of gratitude – an acute awareness of favours to be received); but how else do we realise God's goodness except in the good things he had done? To say that God is good is an abstraction; but God has revealed himself and his goodness to us, not in words nor as an idea, but in practical tokens of his love for us. And on the other hand, it is not servile self-seeking to recognise the gifts of God; on the contrary, it is a mark of nobility to be aware of the goodness of our world. It is a mean-minded person who is never roused to admiration and joy by the sights and sounds and experiences of life. The poet, the artist, or simply the generous-minded person is aware of the beauty and goodness around us. And it is in these experiences that God reveals himself to us.

And our Lord was a person who was aware. We see this continually in his conversation; he is aware of the sky which changes with the seasons, of the flowers, of the crops growing, of the trees rich with leaves and fruit. And in it all he recognises 'the creator of heaven and earth', who makes it yield food, who knows every sparrow that falls, who makes the sun rise and the rain fall.

All of this was in our Lord's mind as he talked to his disciples that last night of his life. And as he talked, his eyes rested on the bread which lay on the table before them, the bread they were eating together. This, this bread, summed up all that was in his heart: God's love, God's love which they shared, God's gift of life, God's continually showered gifts – what better symbol of it all than this bread: 'take it and eat'.

Passover

But this night was not just the eve of our Lord's death, and it was not simply for a last meal together that they were gathered. This was the great Jewish feast of passover, and this was a passover meal.

This feast and this meal had its own theme for 'thanksgiving'. It commemorated the great occasion when Israel came to birth; the first and greatest of God's gifts to Israel, when he led them out of Egypt, from slavery to freedom, from death to life. They remembered how God led them like a shepherd through the desert and fed them with manna. They remembered how God sealed his love for them in a 'covenant', a bond like a marriage bond, a betrothal; there they pledged their love for him and he for them, and gave them his law to lead them to life with him, for 'it is not by bread alone that man lives, but by every word that comes from the mouth of God'. They remembered then the journey to the promised land, the land flowing with milk and honey, the land of peace and joy and happiness where they would live in union with God and in harmony with each other. And every year thereafter the Jews, like our Lord and his disciples, celebrated this event and prayed with faith and hope that God would complete this work of redemption and bring them to perfect freedom and joy.

But this 'celebration' was not merely a passive act of remembering, an act of the imagination by which we project ourselves into the past. It meant reliving the past experience. Israel encountered God in those past events, the exodus, Mount Sinai, the journey through

101

the desert; they experienced his power and goodness. This happened once, and never again; but the ever-living God offered himself to them again with the same power and goodness in their celebration of the event. As they ate the sacred meal, they felt themselves bound in one flesh with their ancestors who had experienced God's salvation, who had eaten the passover meal, who had heard his voice on the mountain – they too were united in covenant with God and with each other.

The true bread

This was the specific occasion of the meal that night; and Jesus's own joyful appreciation of God's gifts of life and friendship merged easily with this more specific theme of national thanksgiving. The bread which was a symbol of his own appreciation of all God's gifts was also the bread of the passover meal, symbol of God's sharing of life with the people he had redeemed.

But God's gifts in creation, God's gifts of mercy, God's gift of salvation to his people – these were not all nor the greatest of God's gifts. The last and greatest of them all was Jesus himself: 'God so loved the world that he sent his son in order that we might have life'. It is hard for us to imagine thanking God for ourselves, that the world has had the privilege of knowing us; but Jesus, knowing who he was and what he was, could do no other. At least once before this he had broken out into such a hymn: 'Thank you, Father, Lord of heaven and earth, for revealing this to little ones – for no one knows the Son except the Father and no one knows the Father except the Son and those to whom the Son reveals him' (Mt 11:25-27). The Lord of heaven and earth – who made the sun and the stars, who shows his fatherly care for us in the fruits of the earth – shows himself even more our Father in the gift of his Son to us; and the Son, brightness of the Father's glory, expression of the Father's love, rejoices that men see the Father in him. And the same spirit runs through his prayer at supper that night (Jn 17) – a spirit of joyful recognition of the Father's love, of his own glory as revealing the Father's love, and the fruit of that love in the gift of life which he shares with men: 'Father, the time has come for you to glorify your Son. All I have is yours, all you have is mine. I have made you known. I have saved those you have given to me. I will share my joy with them. May they be one, as we are one. With me in them and you in me, may they be so completely one that the world may know that it was you who sent me and that I have loved them as much as you love me.'

So the heart and mind and being of Jesus is totally filled with exsultant joy in the contemplation of the whole work of God – not as separate items, as we are bound to consider them, one after the other, but simply as different facets of the Father's glory: his gifts of creation, his gift of salvation, his love for his people whom he bound to himself in a covenant union, and all of this now perfected in the gift of Jesus himself. And all of this together was now summed up in the same symbol – the bread: 'Your fathers ate manna in the desert, but this is the true bread which gives eternal life – take it and eat it; this is my body'.

Given up for you

But human life is not all joy, an unbroken hymn of glad thanksgiving for the gifts showered on us by a loving Father. And Christ's appreciation of life and beauty and love includes a recognition of this aspect of human life too. He as much as anyone recognised that the world we live in is not a paradise; that it brings forth 'thorns and briars' as well as fruit, that it is in the sweat of our brow that we eat bread. He experienced hunger and thirst. 'The son of man had nowhere to lay his head'. He as much as anyone recognised that men do not live as brothers, that they find it as easy to hate their neighbour as to love him.

But in him, this suffering was transmuted and transformed. Instead of being simply the mark of our sinfulness, simply a sign of our separation from God and from each other, it became a sign of even greater love and an even richer life (cf p 40f). Suffering and death became a *sacrifice*. 'Unless the seed falls to the ground and dies, it remains only itself; but if it dies, it brings forth much fruit'. 'Greater love than this no man has, that he should lay down his life'. 'He bore our sorrows . . .' The hour has come for him to suffer the last and greatest agony. But in his heart there was no bitterness, but only supreme love.

The meal which is such a rich symbol of shared life and happiness does not turn sour; the bread does not turn to dust and ashes, the wine does not become gall and vinegar. He gazes at the bread which he still holds in his hands and he sees in it the grain of wheat which falls to the ground and dies, but he sees also the fields white with harvest. 'Take it and eat', he says: 'This is my body which is given up for you'.

Do this in memory of me

All of this was in the mind of Jesus as he ate this last meal with his friends, as he remembered with joy and thanksgiving the love of God for the world – a love that wants life for us, a life that we share with God. He remembered it, and he brought it to perfect fulfilment. No longer would happiness seem like a hopeless mirage, a glimpse of a promised land from which we are cut off by sin – a glimpse which is quickly replaced by the harsh reality of suffering and death. Through him, suffering became the means by which happiness is assured, death became the gateway to a life with God. No wonder he said: 'With desire I have desired to eat this meal with you', and 'When I next eat with you it will be in the kingdom of God'.

We began by pondering on the natural, social significance implicit in any meal; but as we reflect more deeply on *this* meal, we realise that this is more a promise and a hope than a reality, and that the reality of human joy and unity and life is really only achieved in this meal where Christ said, 'Take this and eat it; this is my body'. For Christ really did give us his life, and his Spirit, and his joyful sonship of the Father; he made it possible for men to live as brothers sharing that Spirit and that sonship. Men so united really are his body, living with his life. And in this meal they gather together as a body, with the head of the body, their risen Lord, present in the sacrament of bread.

At mass, then, what are we doing?

First, we are taking part in a meal, a symbol of grateful awareness of life and all that this implies (cf p 100). If we have never enjoyed food and drink, if we have never appreciated God's presence in the world, if we have never known love or beauty, can we really celebrate a *eucharistia*? But we have, and in our celebration we offer all our gifts to God.

Secondly, it is a symbol of unity and harmony, as any meal is. But for christians, this is almost the whole point of our being. Christ came to restore harmony, to make it possible for men to live as brothers; and the first-fruits of that new world was the church, the brotherhood of men who love one another like Christ — and with Christ and in Christ. The church, then, is never more truly itself than in this meal where we renew the bond of unity which *is* the church: 'We are one body, we who share this one bread' (1 Cor 10:17).

But thirdly, the bread we eat is Christ himself. The bread which is the symbol of life – of joy and fulfilment and hope – is the symbol of Christ himself, the perfection of all God's gifts of life; and more than a symbol; it is a sacrament, in which he himself is present to us.[1] He, the risen, glorious, triumphant Lord is life for us, and in eating this bread we are sharing the triumph of him who has conquered death and lives now for God.

And if in the meanwhile life is still imperfect, if suffering and sin and death are still a reality, so too is our share in Christ's sufferings. He made suffering into an act of love, and death the gateway to life. In this meal, we remember (in the fullest sense of the word, p 101), we relive, the sacrifice of Christ – a sacrifice which made it possible for us to do the same and to live the same life. (It is something like a birthday party, in which we celebrate the occasion by which our life began). And in eating this bread, we join ourselves to Christ, we pledge ourselves to make suffering an expression of love, to die if need be for our brethren. We offer ourselves to God like Christ, and with him and in him. Our offering of ourselves is united with his offering of himself as a single offering to the Father.

Note:
1 The Council of Trent in the sixteenth century used the word 'transubstantiation' to describe the fact that through consecration our Lord becomes really present, so that the bread and wine are no longer simply what they appear to be. This term was based on (but not identical with) a view of matter which is difficult to accept today in the present state of atomic physics. Moreover, it tends to suggest a purely physical presence of Christ in the eucharist; whereas Christ himself said, in a context related to the eucharist, 'The flesh profiteth nothing; it is the Spirit which gives life' (Jn 6:63).

This is obviously not the place to go into the philosophical aspects of what we mean by 'real presence', and certainly this is not necessary to grasp and appreciate what we are doing in the eucharist; indeed, excessive concern with this precise problem distorts and obscures more important aspects of the doctrine. We need merely state the two extremes which have to be avoided; we are not dealing here simply with a memorial meal in which the bread and wine merely remind us of our Lord and his work; but on the other hand, it is not the physical Jesus who is magically present in every host, so that the eating of it is a form of cannibalism and there is a miniature Jesus present complete with arms and legs and so on. It is our risen and transfigured Lord who is here.

Appendix – The bible

The bible is the name we give to a fairly large collection of literature – two collections really, which we call the 'old testament' and the 'new testament'. The new testament consists of the four accounts of the work and teaching of our Lord which we call the gospels; an account of the activity of the early church, especially of St Paul, called the Acts of the Apostles; a collection of letters or epistles, especially those of St Paul; and an exhortation to the church in persecution called the Apocalypse. The old testament is a much larger collection of books, all of it dealing with the people of Israel, the Jews; and one reason for putting the two together – later we shall see another reason – is that our Lord was a member of this people, and he and his followers thought of their work as a continuation of the role of Israel.

It is very difficult to sum up the attitude to the bible amongst christians today, because it varies so much; but there are probably two common characteristics: (a) an attitude of reverence and respect: the bible is 'the word of God', it comes to us with the authority of God; if you swear on the bible, you pledge your truth; we speak of something being 'the gospel truth'; but (b) at the same time, many people feel rather bewildered by it; so many things in it, they hear, are not true at all (like the creation of the world in seven days); so many things difficult to believe (like Jonah being swallowed by a whale); so many things difficult to reconcile with the idea of a 'good' book (the brutality and the bloodshed, the treachery and immorality); so many things simply confusing.

This is not the place to go into all of this – many good books are available for those who wish further information and guidance. Here we would like to give a general and basic account of what the bible really is. This in fact may be of some assistance when it comes to dealing with specific problems; but most of all it illustrates what was said above about 'revelation'.

The old testament is the book of the Jewish people; it is a collection of national literature. The history of that people forms the framework of the book. The history begins in a way in the eighteenth century BC, with an account of their ancestors, with Abraham; but the real starting point was the 'exodus', the flight of a group of Hebrews from Egypt followed by a great experience in the south Arabian desert, at mount Sinai; it was from this moment that the people properly so-called takes its origin. They then settled in Palestine (then called Canaan), and eventually adopted a monarchic form of government – the various tribes which composed the people united under a king, David. This event, about 1000 BC, marked the beginning of a golden age for the nation, in power, influence, wealth and culture. This period did not last long; it was only about a century before the nation was split by dissension and coexisted henceforth as two kingdoms. This lasted for about five centuries, when the nation was overwhelmed by the great Mesopotamian power of Babylon, and the most important section of the population was transported to Babylon. This 'exile' lasted for a generation, when the Babylonians were defeated by the Persians, thus allowing the captives to return. This too was an important period in the history, giving them an opportunity to reflect on their past history as they struggled first of all to maintain and then to restore their national existence. They never again reached the status they had achieved in the early days of the monarchy. But though they were always to a greater or lesser extent subject to successive world-powers – Persian, then Greek, then Roman – they never accepted this subjection. There were continual attempts to restore national independence until the Romans in 70 AD put a decisive end to it with the complete destruction of Jerusalem.

This in outline is the history. But Israel regarded themselves as the 'people of God'; they regarded their relationship with God as a 'covenant' – an alliance, by which they had a claim on God and God had a special purpose for them; in the events of their history, then, they saw God at work. They called this 'the word of God' – not a direct speaking, but God acting in their history. They therefore collected their national traditions as a record of what God had done for them (and then of course it becomes 'the word of God' in the other sense, like human words). Of course, the process by which these traditions were handed down and recorded was subject to the same influences as other history and literature. For example, the account of their remote ancestors, Abraham, Isaac and Jacob, and even more the account of the earliest stage of all (the creation, and the stories about mankind before Abraham, contained in the first eleven chapters of the first book of the bible) are not really history at all as we know it. They do not so much describe actual events as they happened, as present a view of the world based on poetic imagination and ancient traditions. They are the equivalent of what in other literature we would call 'myth', except that in Israel's literature they are characterised by a sobriety not often found in most national myths, and by a single-minded concern to express the reality of God's dealings with men.

110

The account of the national history is much more factual, though still, especially in its early stages, based on ancient traditions handed down in different versions, and subject always to the overriding theological concern; the primary purpose is not to give a factual account, 'for the record', but to bring out the work of God.

But besides these traditions concerning the past, Israel's cultural heritage, like that of any other nation, included many other kinds of literature. There were various collections of laws and customs. There was a kind of 'philosophy' – sometimes collections of proverbial sayings embodying the practical wisdom of the people, sometimes longer dialogues (such as the book of Job) dealing with the great problems of human life. There were various kinds of poetry – lyrical, didactic, laments. Most of them were prayers and were collected as the 'Psalms', though there is also the great love poem known as the 'Song of Solomon'. Most striking of all, both in form and content and above all in spirit, are the inspired outpourings of the men called the prophets. These men felt themselves moved, in the very depth of their being, by God, and spoke in the name of God.

This collection of national literature was recognised as expressing and reflecting the character of the nation as the people of God. They are God's people and their book is 'the word of God'.

In the formation of the new testament the same process can be seen – what comes first is the *action* of God: one result of this action is the formation of a community; and it is this community, reflecting on their experience of God, which expresses it in words. In our Lord, God continued and brought to perfection the work which he had done with Israel. 'God spoke to our fathers in various ways at different times through the prophets; and in these last days he has spoken to us

111

through his Son' (Heb 1:1-3). He gathered round him a group of followers, and they, after his death and resurrection, gathered yet others; they called themselves 'the new Israel', the people of God, the people of the new covenant completing and perfecting the covenant with Israel. They then recorded their experience in various ways, the ways we referred to at the beginning. The community, the church, the people of God, the Spirit-filled body of Christ, recognised this record as an authentic expression of their character as the people of God, and this was conserved and handed down to us as the word of God. God does not cease to work in and through his church, his Spirit still speaks to us. But this record composed and authorised by the first followers of Christ, those who had known the word of God in the flesh, has a unique and definitive place in the history of revelation.

But in both the old testament and the new, something very like the incarnation itself takes place; it is something which is at once totally human and totally divine. The bible *is* God's word to us, but not directly, not in a special language, not in words written with God's own hand or spoken by his own mouth. It comes to us in human ways, through the mind of men and in their language and ways of speech, and normal ways of human understanding must be used to grasp it. But through these human means, it is the word of God that comes close to us, confronts us, appeals to us and challenges us.

Further reading

There are so many books available on different aspects of the bible that there is no point in doing more than indicate a few of those which may be useful to start with. A good, clear outline of the principles is given in H. Richards, *God Speaks to Us*, in the *Where We Stand* series which also contains several other short books on various particular parts of the bible. J. Levie, *The Bible, Word of God in Words of Men*, studies the question at somewhat greater length with reference to particular problems. J. L. McKenzie gives a very good explanation of the main points of old testament literature and history in his *Two-Edged Sword*, as he does for the new testament in *The Power and the Wisdom*. Rather more detailed and more comprehensive but still very readable is B. W. Anderson's *Living World of the Old Testament*. For the new testament the same is true of W. H. Davies, *Invitation to the New Testament*. And T. G. A. Baker's *What is the New Testament*, like other SCM Centrebooks, is a good, short way in to the subject. Finally, to mention two books on specific subjects, L. Cerfaux's *The Four Gospels* and C. H. Dodd's *The Meaning of Paul for Today* give the reader a good understanding of these two main parts of the new testament.

113